Praise for *Operation*

This is a poignant and wonderful story of two American women – a story born out of both an instance of America being a force for good in the world, and a terrible tragedy at the very end of the Vietnam War. Follow their journey, their search for answers, their need for closure (and in a very real way – for each other) and enjoy how they become one family. It will warm your heart!

-Rod Bishop, Lt Gen (Ret), USAF

What a truly inspiring book of two strong women who dared to dig deep into their past for healing of the present. It's very touching.

-Carol Hor, Sr. Ursula Lee's Niece

Travel this intriguing journey of sacrifices, love and hope to its beautiful destination of finding and coming home – be it Virginia, Vietnam or within yourself.

-Stephanie Marino, co-editor

This book is incredibly touching and inspiring. It is a vital voice among many from this important time in history.

-Kelly Jackson, Illustrator and Operation Babylift Adoptee

Never have I seen a story evolve with more love, fervor, and sense of family than the written words in this book. I did not want to put it down.

-Ray Snedegar, CMSgt (Ret), USAF, Chief Loadmaster, Operation Babylift C-5A crash survivor

I will share that I have read the book multiple times. Aryn articulated how her life has been formed not only by adoption but by searching for her roots and answers to how she became who she is. Mom (Regina Aune) chronicles her own search for closure to what has been such a traumatic experience. This is a historic account infused with emotion with two different narratives artfully intertwined to tell the story of how the events of April 4, 1975 have impacted so many lives, and how we became a family.

-Diana Taylor, Contract Specialist, Regina Aune's daughter

Aryn and Regina share moving, personal experiences that will edify and inform anyone dealing with adoptive issues or interested in Vietnam War era history. They enlarge the meaning of Mother as they take you with them on their heart-tugging journey of healing. Two lives merge to heal trauma that affected a nation.

- Bonnie Haueter, Artist and Graphic Designer

This book shares the best of human relationships in its pages! The eloquently truthful accounts of these two ladies' lives are truly inspiring and captivating. I feel privileged to have been able to read and know their story. It will make for a great movie!

-Carrie Fox, Military photographer/videographer

"I couldn't put this book down even though I knew many of the details. Operation Babylift:Mission Accomplished *is a story you must read. It is a story of a life-changing tragedy, a story of friendship, love and familial bonding, a story of healing and coming home. The crash of the C-5 during Operation Babylift was a tragedy of huge proportions but its aftermath brought Aryn and Regina experiences they had never dreamed possible. Join them as they embark on a lifetime of discovery, intimacy, joys, sorrows, compassion, healing and growth."*

-Terri Francois M.A., M.Ed., parochial school teacher

Operation Babylift *is a memoir following the two authors on their individual journeys to understand and accept the impact of the plane crash on their lives. From the viewpoint of the crash survivor to that of the orphaned child, this is the story of how the threads of their two lives, linked only by this tragedy, became woven together, binding them in ways that they could never have imagined. Proving that family can be found in the unlikeliest of circumstances, their story reminds us that we should cherish that bond, however and whenever life sends it our way.*

-Christine Richardson, Elementary School Teacher

Operation
Babylift:
Mission Accomplished

A Memoir of Hope and Healing

Thank you for the support.
I hope you enjoy our journey!

by Regina Aune and Aryn Lockhart

Operation Babylift:
Mission Accomplished

Discounts are available for orders of certain quantities. Contact the publisher.

First edition

Designed by Paul Rodriguez

ISBN 978-0-9776906-8-8

Blueline Publishing LLC

1539 Platte Street, Suite 204

Denver, CO 80202 USA

www.bluelinepublishingllc.com

This book is printed on recycled paper.

Dedication

To all my fellow crewmembers from the C-5A inaugural Operation Babylift mission and their families.

Your self-sacrifice will never be forgotten. I carry each of you in my heart.

-Regina Aune

To Sister Mary Agatha Ursula Lee.

My lifelong gratitude for your choices.

To the orphans who never made it home.

-Aryn Lockhart

Table of Contents

Acknowledgements

There are so many people whose lives have crossed my path and influenced the writing of this book that to mention some is to leave me fearful that I will fail to mention others who should be remembered. I am grateful for all those individuals who have been and are a part of my life and who have in so very many ways had a part to play in writing this book.

First and foremost, I want to thank my late husband, Bjorn. He shared every step of this journey with me and was my strongest supporter, my best friend, and the love of my life. Our nearly 38 years of marriage were the happiest years of my life. He so very much wanted to see this book written. He certainly was a significant part of this writing journey, and both Aryn and I know that he was with us as we wrote. I am sad that he is not here to read the final fruit of our writing. I miss you every day and will love you always, my tender Norwegian Bear!

My daughters, Ellen, Diana, and Elizabeth endured all the moves, uncertainties, wonders, and frustrations of being "military brats." I could not have written this book without their encouragement and their love. Thanks, girls, I will always love each of you!

My daughter of the heart, Aryn – there are no words to express my thanks and gratitude for all that you have given me, and not only me, but all of us Aunes. Our lives have been enriched greatly because you are a part of them. I cannot imagine my life without you as a part of it. I will love you always!

Ray Snedegar, what can I say? I am so very glad you joined us on our trip to Vietnam. You will never know how much your presence and participation in our Vietnam adventure meant and how it helped me in countless ways. But even more, our friendship, begun in the debris-strewn wreckage of the C-5 in the rice paddies of Saigon forty years ago, is a priceless pearl that I treasure in my heart for always. (You really don't remember keeping our car at your house, waxing and polishing it, while I was in the hospital at Clark?!)

I also want to thank Father Richard Novotny for so graciously making his house available to Aryn and me as we began our work of writing. His encouragement was invaluable and his hospitality exceptional. (Thanks, too, for indulging my whim and taking us to Belgium so I could get some Belgian mayonnaise!)

I am indebted to Helen Antonelli for graciously reading and critiquing the draft. Her thoughtful comments and suggestions as well as her insights were a gift to me and helped me to express my thoughts clearly and completely. I will be ever grateful to her for her generosity and, more importantly, for her friendship.

As our days of writing became more intense and the crush of deadlines approached, Father Charles Khachan, MLM, and my St. George Maronite Catholic parish family gave me encouragement and support in ways that I know they do not even realize. A simple thank you seems so inadequate. Each of you is a unique blessing to me and I am so grateful that you are a part of my life.

St. Rafqa, you were always there to help us find what was lost while we traveled in Vietnam. I am and will be eternally grateful to you for your intercession during our travels and beyond.

And last, but most certainly not least, I thank God for the life and the talents that he has given me. He has richly blessed my life and, whether in moments of sadness and sorrow or in moments of happiness and joy, his grace always has been there for me. His Divine Providence has sustained me always and I pray and trust that it always will.

-Regina Aune

I feel that there is a vast list of those I would like to thank in my efforts to write this book. I have received encouragement throughout the years to persevere, so to finally place the last period leaves me with feelings of complete fulfillment and some sadness. My journey to write and pour myself onto these pages has been emotional at times. It has been a very deliberate, heartfelt offering full of vulnerabilities scattered along the path.

As I feel this book is a tale of gratitude, it is important for me to take the time to recognize some significant influences.

First and foremost, I need and want to thank my parents. Upon my arrival and through the harrowing events surrounding my earliest days, you created the foundation of my character. You define the importance of nurture. It was through your willingness to open your home and heart, that I have been afforded amazing opportunities and have come to recognize the importance of choices. It is from you that I learned the value of love. I am and will always be grateful to be your daughter.

In that same light, while I have written this story with my San Antonio (SA) Mom, I feel I need to take the time to thank both her and my SA Dad. I never imagined our initial meeting would culminate in this amazing story of our lives and our paths becoming one. I am so glad we made our dreams a reality, both in our return to Vietnam together and in the process of writing this book. SA Dad, though not physically here, was very much with us throughout our writing and he is always in my heart. Thank you for embracing me into your life and the Aune clan with such genuine and amazing love.

I'd also like to thank my husband, Martin. There were many months where our normal routine was significantly altered. You worked with me throughout the process, allowing me the focus necessary to find the words to tell my story. I am truly thankful that you accompanied me to Vietnam and through this intensely emotional journey. While you're not the most emotional guy, you were always there to offer a tissue on my behalf and I knew it was your heartfelt way to support me.

Additionally, I'd like to thank Ray Snedegar, the loadmaster and a survivor of the C-5 crash. I am so thankful that you decided to join us on our trip to Vietnam. In addition to my relationship with SA Mom, my relationship with you is bonded by the heart. I believe our trip back to Vietnam was healing for all of us. I feel truly connected to you and I am so glad our paths crossed. I love you too much, Ray.

I deeply appreciate my San Antonio sisters for their contributions. It was eye-opening to read your perspectives in your own words. I am touched by your honesty and loving thoughts. I am always grateful for your love and acceptance.

I'd like to thank Father Richard Novotny, who allowed my SA Mom and me to hide away at his home in Bitburg, Germany to start our writing adventure. Allowing us the isolation to focus and begin our story set us on our path to success.

I also thank and acknowledge Colonel Nick Pratt. When Nick learned of my story, every time he crossed my path, he would ask about the book's progress. He passed away suddenly in December of 2013, but his encouragement and persistence were with me throughout the book. I am ever grateful for his guidance and warm encouragement. Hey Nick, I finally did it. Semper Fi.

Last, but far from least, I'd like to thank Stephanie Marino. Partly by accident, I had the good fortune of choosing you to help me edit and polish my words. In addition to providing your comprehensive edits, you also played the vital role of encouragement and focus throughout the writing process. With your guidance, I am certain my story took on greater depth and clarity. You are invaluable. Thank you for helping me find my voice.

-Aryn Lockhart

Foreword

We wept. We held onto one another tightly, and we wept uncontrollably. We stood in a rice paddy thousands of miles from home in Vietnam on hallowed ground where so many innocent people had lost their lives nearly 40 years prior, and we wept. Two of us were the most outwardly showing our emotions, as we watched a civilian airline banking into its final approach to the Saigon (now Ho Chi Minh City) airport, and our minds went back to a C-5A 80218 starting that final approach on 4 April 1975 that didn't make it. We had been on that flight. We stood on the ground where carnage had been long ago, and we wept.

There is a common phrase that states, "Friends are the family you choose for yourself." Never have I seen a story evolve with more love, fervor, and sense of family than the one written in this book. I met both Aryn Lockhart and Regina Aune for the very first time on 4 April 1975 on a day that became history in a very tragic way.

That day started for Regina and me as a day of excitement and hope, since we were flying a mission for humanitarian reasons to rescue Amerasian babies and children from the perils of war and its aftermath in South Vietnam as the North Vietnamese advanced, conquering the South.

BOOM! That loud bang as we were climbing toward 14,000 feet altitude out of Saigon with more than 300 souls onboard resulted in a large part of the tail section being blown off the C-5A and in an instantaneous rapid decompression. Many persons were lost in this accident and numerous others injured.

This story is about two ladies who survived this crash and how their lives have intertwined since that fateful day. One lady, Aryn, was an infant on the plane; the other one, Regina, was a young Air Force Officer Flight Nurse who was Chief Medical Director on the flight. Aryn knew from an early age that she was a part of Operation Babylift but had limited knowledge of who she really was and what had happened. She sought out Regina after reading an article about her role on that day in an Air Force publication twenty-plus years after that tragic day in 1975. This story is about the friendship, adventures, and life-changing moments of these two since Aryn reached out to Regina for answers. Regina and I have been in contact regularly since that fateful day we first met but I had never met Aryn until Regina's retirement from the Air Force in late 2006. That was the beginning of a new inseparable bond and friendship.

I know this story because I was a part of it also. I was the Chief Loadmaster on that flight crew for this Operation Babylift mission and have been included in both ladies' lives over the years since. They are two incredible women of faith who have formed a bond beyond description since that tragic moment in their lives.

I was elated when they asked me to accompany them back to Vietnam in November 2014 to help Aryn try to capture some sense of her culture and look for answers in her life. I am proud of these ladies; I am proud to be called their friend, and want them to know I love them both. It is true that friends are the family you choose for yourself. We are three fortunate persons. We are family.

-Ray Snedegar, CMSgt (Ret), USAF

1

The End and the Beginning

Aryn and I had wanted to tell our story of how Operation Babylift played a pivotal role in our lives. In planning and writing the book, we wanted you the reader to meet us as individuals but also to understand how our lives intersected. Thus, the book is written in each of our own voices – sometimes in Aryn's and sometimes in mine, but always connected so that you can see how events in our lives were experienced by each of us. The experience of writing this book together has served to make our bond of love and family even stronger than it was before we began this adventure. It is our story in our words.

-Regina

Regina:

It is Sunday, 23 November 2014, and I am ensconced in Aryn's living room in Garmisch, Germany as I write these words. I am still trying to make sense of our trip to Vietnam – a trip that was happily planned and eagerly anticipated for so many years – a trip that truly did not disappoint. It began on 31 October when we flew to Vietnam, and it ended on Thursday, 20 November at 6:15 am when our Etihad flight from Abu Dhabi landed in Munich. Where to begin? I have so many thoughts tumbling and crashing into each other in my head that I do not know how to sort them out let alone express them intelligently and coherently. Aryn and I have always believed that we needed to make a trip to Vietnam in order to tell the story that unfolds in the subsequent pages of this book. That was and is very true.

As eagerly as we planned the trip and saw those plans come to fruition, both the planning and the execution were fraught with anxiety for me. I love to travel and always look forward to trips that I plan. But this trip was qualitatively different from any other trip I had planned or undertaken. I did not know what to expect or how I would feel about returning to Vietnam. It was as if there were two Reginas sparring over the trip. One Regina eagerly planned and dreamed about the trip and the other Regina was feverishly seeking a way to disengage gracefully from going.

Vietnam has always been present in my mind and heart ever since that hot, humid April day in 1975 when an unusual aeromedical evacuation mission turned into a tragedy of horrific proportions. Every image, every sound, every smell, every possible sensory experience and every thought I had on April 4, 1975, is etched forever into my memory. They are there because I cannot forget them and because I do not want to forget them. I hold fast to them because they are a part of me – of who I am and who I have become. My fear is that if I forget them, I will lose a part of who I am.

Aryn, Martin (Aryn's husband), Ray (one of the loadmasters on the C-5), and I arrived in Vietnam in the evening of 5 November. We had decided that the first thing we would do the next day was visit the C-5 crash site. After several attempts to find the actual site, we were directed down a path by one of the local villagers who said it led to the crash site. As anxious as I was to see the site, I was also apprehensive. As we started down the path, I recognized it for what it was, even though it did not look like it had 40 years earlier. The landscape had changed. No longer were there endless rice paddies. But the trough of water between the rows of vegetation reminded me of them. Now there were trees and a barn and a path from the road where the car was parked. The road had not existed in 1975. There was an almost surreal aspect to the moment. In an instant, I was transported back to that April day when I stepped out of the wrecked C-5 and surveyed the destruction and devastation all around me. Looking at the scene now, I saw not what was really before me but rather what I saw on that April day so long ago. And at the same time I saw the land as it was in the present moment. Everything had changed, yet everything was the same. How could things be so peaceful now when they were anything but, on that fateful day? How could the world have continued when it seemed it had stopped on April 4, 1975?

After looking at the ground for some time, I heard the sound of an airplane overhead. Although the plane was not a C-5, the sound reminded me of the whine of the C-5 engines. I hear them all the time at home in San Antonio, but the memory evoked by the sound of the plane's engines took me deeper into my reverie, and I listened to the sound as though I were hearing it for the first time. I turned and looked up at the sky and saw the plane on approach to Tan Son Nhut Airport – the same Tan Son Nhut where we had landed only the day before, the same Tan Son Nhut where we had landed 40 years before, the same Tan Son Nhut where we had departed with so much hope, only to have those hopes dashed and buried in the mud of the rice paddies. How had so much time elapsed? How could things look so different and yet the same? Things were so tranquil and normal now but they certainly weren't on that long-ago April day. The peacefulness of the moment contrasted sharply with my memories of that earlier time. Try as I might, I could not reconcile what I was experiencing now with what I had experienced 40 years earlier. The dissonance was frustrating. I was without words to explain what I was feeling at that moment and I have no words to explain it now. All I know is that my life was forever changed by a flight that lasted less than 20 minutes.

As clearly etched as those memories are, has time distorted them? I don't think so. But time has a way of maturing thought and memory, and how I perceive things now is different from how I perceived events then. At the time of the crash all I could think about, all that I perceived, was the tremendous loss of life that resulted. Though that hasn't changed, I no longer look at the crash as such an overwhelming loss. Rather, while I continue to see the loss of life on that day as tragic, that loss has been tempered by what I have gained and what I have been given, but these are my initial thoughts. Aryn's thoughts are similar but unique as well. I was an adult, but she was a baby and has no recollection of the day that she left the country of her birth.

Aryn:

Operation Babylift. My mind has created images based on yellowing newspapers and dated film footage that I've seen in a few documentaries. These two words defined my journey to America. My history was made up of newspaper articles covering the 5Ws of Who, What, When, Where and Why.

On April 2, 1975, President Gerald Ford announced the humanitarian mission known as Operation Babylift. The mission's sole purpose was to transport out of Vietnam approximately two thousand orphans who were already in the process of being adopted. The state of South Vietnam was deteriorating rapidly. The North Vietnamese appeared to be fast approaching, and there were great concerns regarding the Communist regime and who would suffer under their rule. The orphans were on the forefront of many people's minds.

"I have directed money from a $2 million special foreign aid children's fund be made available to fly 2,000 South Vietnamese orphans to the United States as soon as possible," President Ford announced at a press conference. "I have directed that C-5A aircraft especially equipped to care for these orphans be sent to Saigon. I expect these flights to begin in the next 36 to 48 hours."

I watched dated film footage with dusty and shaky images capturing this historical event. Scores of people with babies in hand filed onto this large cargo plane, then used ties and large straps as makeshift seat belts. I gazed upon history, trying to imagine the chaos of that day. The documentary then shifts as I see aerial footage shortly after the crash with the C-5 in pieces strewn throughout the rice paddies. I looked at unknown pieces and parts of the aircraft, unable to distinguish one from the other. I saw wet, muddy fields and twisted, mangled metal – all remnants of the monstrous aircraft. My newspaper articles depicted a black cloud of smoke rising from the pieces of the wreckage and horrified faces of staff watching as charred bodies were brought past them at the hospital.

I was just watching a movie – a moment and a glimpse into history. Yet this movie was different. I was looking back in time to what I believed was my history. I was a baby from Operation Babylift. On April 4, 1975, 138 lives were lost, including the nun who had chosen me for my parents. This mission was filled with hope and so much of that hope died in the wreckage of a muddy rice field.

Forty years later, I stood in this same field with two surviving crew members at my side. I had returned to my homeland, and these pages describe my life's journey, which brought me full circle.

2

Regina's Story

On my wall above the desk in my work area at home is a framed picture with the saying, "Coincidences are God's way of letting you know he is paying attention." Many things and events that have happened in my life might be labeled coincidences. However, I prefer to look at these things and events as special moments when Divine Providence touched my heart and soul in a very direct way. Looking back on the whole of my life, God's providence was and always has been there, even if I did not see it or acknowledge it at the time. The story told in the pages of this book is the story of the continuous unfolding of that providence in my life as well as in the lives of those whom I love.

My story begins in Ohio. I was born in Lakewood, a suburb of Cleveland, and I grew up in those areas. When I lived there I did not always appreciate the richness of the city or the interplay of its rich cultural life – a blend of West and East European immigrants who worked, played, and lived together in harmony. Cleveland is not a pretty city in the way some cities are pretty, not like Charleston or Savannah. It is not a city that invites visitors from around the world like New York or San Francisco. It had been a steel city, bearing with it all the grunge and grime that is part of an industrial city. It is no longer an industrial city, and in many ways it is a tired city. But, it had its own charm, its symphony, its museums and its theaters, its parks and its playgrounds, its rich and its poor.

The city was a city of contrasts and yet a melting pot of peoples. The Jewish deli down the street was the best place to get dill pickles from the barrel, the Russian Orthodox Cathedral was not far from where I lived, I heard Polish and Greek and Italian and Russian and a whole variety of languages spoken in the shops in my neighborhood, and it was possible to find newspapers in all those languages at the corner grocery store. I walked past the Byzantine Catholic school to go to my own Latin Catholic school, composed mostly of children of German and Irish immigrants with some Polish, Czech and Hungarian mixed in for good measure. My friends were Greek Orthodox, Syrian Catholic, Russian Orthodox, Jewish, Lutheran, Italian, German, French, Irish, Polish, Czech, Greek – a veritable smorgasbord of nationalities, religions and cultures. I enjoyed eating pierogies and pizzelles and matzo as much as I enjoyed hamburgers and hot dogs.

If you lived in Cleveland or Lakewood, you lived near "the lake." Of course, "the lake" was Lake Erie, and sitting on the water's edge looking across its 50-mile-wide expanse, I always thought of Canada and my desire to travel. I cannot remember a time when I did not want to see more of the world, live in other places, meet other people, travel to other countries, always wanting to enlarge and expand my understanding of both people and the world. These ideas were nurtured and encouraged by my parents, who always nudged my brother and me to follow our dreams and move beyond the cocoon of our childhood.

My family, on both my mother's side and my father's side, had a proud tradition of service to the nation beginning with the Revolutionary War. Indeed, my ancestors had come to America before there was either an America (as we know it today) or a United States. Although my ancestry is German, Swiss, French, Irish, English, Scotch and Dutch, I am far removed from the status of an immigrant. My family has lived in the United States since the 1600s. My father and his brothers all served in the Army Air Corps during World War II, and my brother and I grew up listening to their "war stories" and absorbing, almost by osmosis, their patriotism and love for America. Love of country and patriotism had been nurtured by their parents and their grandparents and their grandparents' parents and grandparents all the way back to the beginnings of the country as a nation. It was not a blind patriotism but rather a realistic love for country that inspired my family to serve and preserve what had been won at such great cost. It was that educated patriotism instilled in my brother and me by our parents that played a significant part in my brother's decision to enlist in the Marine Corps and in my decision to seek a commission in the Air Force.

I graduated with my nursing degree from St. John College of Cleveland, a small Catholic diocesan women's college nestled in the shadow of the cathedral and the chancery on Ninth Street and Superior Avenue in downtown Cleveland. It no longer exists, but it prepared me well for all the challenges that I would meet as a person and as a nurse. It was there that I learned the skills of nursing and the art of caring for the sick. But even more than the nursing skills I learned there, I received a classical liberal arts education, an education that taught me to think, to reason, and to ask the fundamental questions about life and its purpose.

My college education continued teaching me what it meant to be a Catholic in the world, a process that began in first grade and continued throughout all my years of education through my undergraduate years. My parents had begun that education even before I began school and certainly they were the primary influence on the development of my character and the primary shapers of who I have become today. It was this solid formation in the Catholic faith that influenced me and became an integral part of my life. Today it is fashionable to discuss the foibles and the "horror stories" of Catholic schools, but I harbor no regrets about my Catholic education and I am grateful for what it taught me and what I received from it. In no small measure it is because of the solid foundation of my education by my parents and by my formal education in the Catholic schools I attended that I am the person I am.

My first year after graduation I worked in Warren, Ohio at a small Catholic hospital situated near the banks of the Mahoning River. It was here that I learned truly what it meant to be a nurse without the safety net of instructors and college professors. It was here too that I faced for the first time the heart-breaking, gut-wrenching realities of life. On my very first day as a brand new nurse, I found myself assigned to work in the Emergency Room.

My first day also became one of the saddest days of my nursing career. I had barely received an orientation to the location of all the equipment and supplies, briefly met the other nurses assigned to the Emergency Room, and was given my assignment for the day (which really was to shadow another nurse), when a young boy was brought to the Emergency Room by the Fire Department, unconscious and barely breathing, an apparent drowning victim. The boy's parents were on their way to the hospital, and the head nurse told me to meet them and take them to a small waiting room off the Emergency Room. I did so, and for the first time in my life faced the intense grief of a mother who had to deal with the unanticipated and unexpected death of her 12-year-old son by drowning. She kept asking me to tell her it wasn't true and then asked me why this had happened. There are and were no textbook answers to those questions; rather, helping this mother in her grief required entering into her very palpable pain and anguish with an empathy born of genuine care and concern for her. As I talked to her, I cried with her, not only because I shared her suffering but also because I wondered if I was equal to the challenge that the nursing profession is on a daily basis. I wondered if I had made a mistake in choosing to become a nurse. I felt so inadequate in that moment. I faced even more heartbreaking situations throughout that first year. But, I gained confidence in my skills and abilities to handle whatever situations were presented to me, and found that in choosing nursing as a profession I had not made a mistake.

I had always wanted to be a teacher. In my early elementary school years and even into the first year or so of high school, I planned on going to college to prepare myself to be an English and history teacher. But, at some point, the idea of becoming a nurse crept into my thoughts and I pondered just what my future career should be. The genesis for these thoughts of nursing surely had their origins in my work with the physically handicapped and mentally challenged children at the Rosemary Home in Cleveland. On Saturdays throughout the school year and on additional weekdays during summer breaks while I was in high school, I worked as a volunteer at the Rosemary Home, a facility operated by the Sisters of the Humility of Mary and the same religious community to which my high school teachers belonged. I loved working with the children. They taught me invaluable lessons about what it is to be truly human and they gave me much more than I ever gave them; their determination, their cheerfulness, their simplicity, their joy despite their physical and/or mental challenges touched the deepest recesses of my heart. And, I loved working with the Sisters. Their joyful self-giving in caring for these children was an inspiration to me and reinforced to me the inherent dignity and worth of every human life, made in the image of God.

But I never lost my desire to teach. In my second year as a nurse, I had the opportunity to teach in a diploma nursing program in Youngstown, Ohio. I spent two years at the school teaching freshmen and junior students nursing skills and what was required to learn the art of nursing.

★ ★ ★

The Vietnam War was still raging and dividing the nation in ways that are unimaginable today. My brother had enlisted in the Marine Corps, and after assignments to Camp LeJeune, North Carolina, and Kaneohe,

Hawaii, he was assigned to Vietnam as a Marine advisor to South Vietnamese troops. The experiences he shared with us in letters and phone calls and infrequent leave times were the impetus that made me begin to think about military nursing as an option. But I did not know to which of the three nurse corps – Army, Navy, or Air Force – to apply for a commission. I was intrigued by flight nursing and so I was somewhat partial to the Air Force. The fact that my father and his brothers had all served in the Army Air Corps (which later became the Air Force) also influenced the direction of my thinking.

My brother was still serving as a Marine advisor to the South Vietnamese troops when I wrote him a letter and asked him for his thoughts and advice about my desire to become a military nurse and which service I should choose. I will never forget his opening remarks in his letter to me. He wrote:

> *Dear Gina,*
>
> *Greetings from the hell hole of the world! I have read your letter and think what you want to do is great and a good opportunity for you. . .*

In that letter, he told me that he thought I would probably find the Air Force the most satisfying service and because I was already interested in the flight nursing opportunities that the Air Force offered, it made the most sense to apply to the Air Force. Even today, I always tell everyone that I became an Air Force officer because a Marine told me to do it. I don't always tell people that the Marine was my brother!

Thus, on 5 January 1973, I found myself on a Braniff Airlines flight to Dallas, Texas, en route to Sheppard Air Force Base (AFB) in Wichita Falls, Texas, to begin Military Indoctrination for Medical Service Officers (MIMSO), the basic orientation course for all new officers in the medical services of the Air Force. The course was a brief two weeks and barely scratched the surface of what being an officer in the military entailed. The two weeks I spent at MIMSO were made even more interesting by the unusual weather we endured. The first week we had an ice storm and everything froze, walking anywhere was nearly impossible, and most of us had to deal with missing luggage that didn't appear until about our fifth day at the base. The freezing temperatures caused many of the water lines to burst and when the temperatures rose to the 70s and higher during the second week, the frozen terrain turned into enormous piles of muddy sludge that made walking anywhere just as impossible as the ice had made it the previous week.

Our last night of what we had begun to call "military play school" was celebrated at an official "Dining In," a social gathering of military members which has specific rules of engagement (some of them quite amusing) with the sole purpose of enhancing military camaraderie. I do not remember the name of the colonel who was the speaker at the Dining In but I do remember what he said. In short, he told us that as members of the military we were going to have many opportunities that most of our fellow Americans would never have and it was incumbent upon us to make sure that we conveyed what we learned from those experiences to our fellow countrymen. And, likewise, we were to be true ambassadors of what was best in America to those citizens of other countries whom we would encounter in our assignments and travels. Ultimately, our mission was to build peace in the world through the ordinary events of life wherever we were. As military members we were to be the exemplars of what is good in humanity.

The following day we all departed for our initial assignments. (Today, the new officers in the medical services undergo a more rigorous and longer orientation and introduction to what is expected of a military officer and what it means to be an officer. Their military orientation is at Maxwell AFB in Alabama and no longer at Sheppard AFB.)

My first assignment as an Air Force nurse was to Malcolm Grow Medical Center at Andrews AFB in Maryland. Seven of us who had attended MIMSO together were assigned to Andrews, and we arrived there around 20 January. As I mentioned, our MIMSO course did not begin to enlighten us regarding what was expected of us as officers and nurses in the Air Force, but we were fortunate to have excellent senior nurses who mentored us in an exceptional way and helped us learn how to be military officers. Some of these nurses had been in the Army immediately after World War II and had transferred to the Air Force when the Air Force Medical Service was created in 1949. They were well-versed in all things military and understood the military inside and out. They certainly understood how very naive we lieutenants were about all things military.

In addition to teaching us how things worked in the medical service, they taught us all the customs and courtesies peculiar to the military, enlarged our view of the military beyond the medical service, and provided correction with understanding when we breached some particular aspect of military protocol. I am sure that they had many moments of mirth, laughing at our foibles as lieutenants. Lieutenants are the "wide-eyed children" of the military and can be forgiven for doing ridiculous things such as parking in a spot marked "General Officer" because they think it means any officer when it really means a general; many things lieutenants do very early in their careers are done out of ignorance and not malice. That was assuredly the case with my peer group of lieutenants in 1973.

A week after my arrival at Andrews, on 27 January 1973, the Paris Peace Accords were signed and a cease fire was declared, effectively ending the war in Vietnam. The U.S. Senate never signed the accords and the fighting did not stop completely. Although the total withdrawal of U.S. troops and the cessation of fighting by the North and the South were critical elements of the agreement, hostilities did continue and some U.S. forces, though radically reduced in number, remained in South Vietnam.

On 13 February 1973, the first repatriated Prisoners of War (POWs) arrived at Clark Air Base (AB) in the Philippines on a C-141 aircraft. Various military medical centers had already been designated to receive the POWs when they arrived back in the states and Malcolm Grow was one of the designated facilities. The hospital was a nexus of activity in preparation for the POWs' arrival. Although I was not one of the nurses designated to work with the POWs, toward the end of the six weeks that they were at the facility I was transferred to the unit where they had been treated. Most of them had been discharged from the hospital but several were still there, and I had an opportunity to interact with them. It was a memorable time for me because they so willingly shared what they had learned from the experience. To a man, and despite all that they had suffered while imprisoned in Vietnam, they exuded a nobility of spirit, an undying faith in the goodness of people, and a genuine love for the country despite the moments when they feared they had been abandoned to their ugly fate. Their strength of character and their steadfastness in the face of extreme adversity was a powerful and influential example to me as I began my military career.

My first year in the Air Force was a mixture of highs and lows, monotony and excitement, meeting new friends and keeping up with old friends – the usual experiences of learning to adjust and adapt to the vicissitudes of a military career and living in a new location. Toward the end of my first year in the Air Force, one of my fellow nurses and I took three weeks of leave and traveled Space Available (Space A) to Europe. Space A travel is one of the benefits of being in the military. Space A travel refers to the ability to travel on a military plane to a destination when there is space available on the aircraft and at no cost to the traveler. We traveled on a plane from the 89th Wing at Andrews to Rhein Main AB, Germany and from there made our way through Bavaria, Austria, Greece, Italy and Spain, before we returned home on a C-5 aircraft.

In May 1974, I headed to Brooks AFB in San Antonio, Texas, to attend the flight nurse course – a step in realizing my dream of becoming an Air Force flight nurse. I was the only active duty student in the class who had a follow-on assignment to an aeromedical evacuation squadron. The five weeks of class were exhausting and intense. In addition to the aerospace nursing content, the course included water survival and basic survival training as well as "flights" in the altitude chamber, classroom activities, equipment skills verification, and training flights over the Gulf of Mexico. The intensity of the course could not check my enthusiasm for flight nursing nor dampen the exhilaration I experienced while at school. I could hardly wait to go to my flying assignment!

At the conclusion of the course in July, I took 14 days of leave to visit my brother who then was assigned to the Marine Corps Recruit Depot in San Diego, California. My original orders for my flying assignment were to McGuire AFB in New Jersey, but while I was visiting my brother, the orders were changed and I was assigned to the 10th Aeromedical Evacuation Squadron (AES) at Travis AFB in Fairfield, California.

The usual mission for the 10th AES was to fly from Clark AB in the Philippines through Andersen AFB, Guam, and Hickam AFB, Hawaii, to Travis AFB. In late fall of 1974, the Air Force began the process of consolidating the Aeromedical Evacuation Squadrons (AES) on the east and west coasts with their respective AES counterparts in Germany and the Philippines. In January 1975, the squadrons began the integration process by flying each others' missions.

The 10th AES was qualified to fly aeromedical evacuation missions on C-141 and C-9 aircraft, although the 10th AES's primary aircraft was the C-141. The C-141 Starlifter was a large, long-range cargo aircraft capable of carrying cargo or troops or both. The 9th AES, which was located at Clark AB in the Philippines, flew only on the C-9. The C-9 Nightingale was a specially configured aircraft that was designed specifically for the transport of patients and was used exclusively for aeromedical evacuation missions.

My life in 1974 and early 1975 was not wholly consumed with flying and the Air Force. While I had been assigned to Andrews, I met my future husband, Bjorn. He also was assigned to Malcolm Grow and we began dating in 1974. But, as often happens in the military, I received orders for flight school and the follow-on assignment to the aeromedical evacuation squadron and he received orders to Kadena AB in Okinawa, Japan. He formally proposed to me in a telephone call from Okinawa in September, 1974, and we managed to see each other one weekend in November while I was at Clark. He gave me my engagement ring during that short visit and we planned a June wedding. We saw each other only those five days during the time we were engaged and that was on his short trip to the Philippines. (Our phone bills are another story!)

Our wedding actually occurred at the chapel at Travis AFB on 8 February 1975. With the consolidation of the aeromedical evacuation squadrons, I received orders to the Philippines and his tour in Okinawa was going to be curtailed. Had we waited until June to get married, we probably would have been geographically separated for the first several years of our marriage! The military chaplain who was working with us on our wedding plans agreed to allow us to move the wedding from June to February so that Bjorn could apply for a joint spouse move to the Philippines.

I must have been the 1975 version of the "Energizer Bunny" because not only was I flying aeromedical evacuation missions between Travis AFB and the Philippines, but I made my wedding dress and the bridesmaids' dresses, in addition to arranging for the catering at the Officers' Club for the reception, addressing and mailing all the wedding invitations, finding hotel rooms for all the guests coming from out of town (which was just about everyone!), and handling all the myriad small details that are part of any wedding.

★ ★ ★

While the Air Force busied itself with the integration of squadrons in the aeromedical evacuation arena, world history marched forward. The stability of South Vietnam was becoming a serious problem as North Vietnamese soldiers made multiple incursions into the South and villages were quickly taken by the North Vietnamese. There were seven organizations that worked with the orphanages in South Vietnam in arranging placement and adoptions for the children under their care. As the situation in South Vietnam continued to destabilize, these agencies sought assistance from the U.S. government in moving these children to waiting families in the United States, Australia, Canada, and Europe. Amid growing concern regarding the long-term sustainment of South Vietnam as a nation and anxiety regarding the fate of the children in the orphanages, President Ford ordered Operation Babylift.

I was on leave for most of the month of February because of our wedding and honeymoon. I returned to flying the first of March, and while I was on alert at Hickam for C-141 urgent missions, I flew to Australia to pick up a patient and brought her and her family back to Hickam. I returned to Travis, had a few days of crew rest and then was scheduled to fly back to Clark in the Philippines on 30 March (Easter Sunday). Prior to our departure for Clark (there was an entire medical crew departing for Clark), our chief nurse had briefed us on the deteriorating conditions in Vietnam and told us that we were to report to both our 10th AES detachment at Clark and the 9th AES chief nurse upon our arrival. The five of us were actually scheduled to be in the Philippines for the entire month of April flying regularly scheduled C-9 missions and pulling alert for urgent C-141 missions.

Our flight to the Philippines was uneventful and routine. We arrived at 0600 (6:00 am) on Tuesday morning, 1 April. (A day was always "lost" when arriving at Clark from Travis because of crossing the International Date Line.) The chief nurse briefed us on the situation in Vietnam as it was known at the time. She gave us our schedule for the week and indicated that there was a possibility of not only changes to the schedule but also the addition of some flights to Saigon (now Ho Chi Minh City). I was scheduled to pull alert for C-141 urgent missions from Thursday morning, 3 April, until Friday morning, 4 April, and then fly a three-day mission to Thailand, Korea, and Japan after that. (Alerts were from 8:00 am one morning until 8:00 am the next morning.)

The ringing of the phone in my room at the Chambers Hall Bachelor Officers' Quarters (BOQ or lodging facility) on the morning of 4 April jarred me awake at 6:00 am. The alert call was not only for me as the C-141 alert nurse but for all of us nurses staying in the BOQ who were assigned to the 10th AES. The message was simply that we would be flying missions to Saigon and the crew bus would pick us up and take us to the 9th AES in 15 minutes! With all of the nurses and technicians of the 9th AES and what members of my squadron were available at Clark AB, I reported to the 9th AES's briefing room wondering what the day's flying duties would entail and which aircraft would be used to fly to Saigon. All of us shared coffee and conversation. Uncertainty about our prospective missions dominated the small talk while we waited for information and assignments.

After what seemed a very long time, the chief nurse identified a medical crew composed of nurses and medical technicians from the 9th AES to fly on a C-9. However, a short time later, she returned to the briefing room and stated that the mission to Saigon would be on a C-5 Galaxy and therefore a different medical crew was selected for the mission. I was selected to be the Medical Crew Director; the new crew was composed of members of the 9th AES, the 10th AES, and the 65th AES (the Reserve AES at Travis). There was no further information available regarding the mission. Because the organizations working with the orphanages in Saigon had requested assistance, we assumed we would be transporting children. I was surprised and momentarily overwhelmed by my assignment. Nonetheless, we hastily gathered supplies and equipment needed for an aeromedical evacuation mission and left for the flight line.

After arriving at the aircraft, the medical crew and the flight crew introduced themselves. I will never forget the aircraft commander's introduction. He said, "Hi, I'm Bud Traynor and I have never flown an air evac mission!" Normally, the medical crew director gives a briefing to the aircraft commander regarding the particular patient population for the mission and whether any special equipment will be used in flight. And, the aircraft commander gives a briefing regarding the anticipated mission in terms of weather, altitude, and other information pertaining to the flight that might have an impact on the patients. But, for this particular mission, neither crew knew exactly what would be involved. However, C-5s had never been used for aeromedical evacuation missions, so the medical crew needed to learn the peculiarities of the C-5 while enroute to Saigon. Once we were airborne, the flight crew provided the medical crew with a tour and walking lesson on the features of the C-5. (Needless to say, we had no checklist for a C-5.)

Chaos is the only word that can describe the scene on the flight line after landing at Tan Son Nhut AB in Saigon. Planes were everywhere: C-130s from Australia, C-130s of the South Vietnamese Air Force, U.S. planes, European planes. Aside from the chaos, the heat was stifling. The C-5 was parked just off the runway. The noise from the constant traffic on the runway blended with the hot, humid conditions of the day and the smells of jet engine fuel. Bathed in sweat, I felt as though I were eating all the grime and dirt of the airfield. From the ramp of the C-5, I watched the activities swirling about the field. Even after the cargo was off-loaded from the plane, our particular aeromedical evacuation mission still eluded us. The flight crew and the medical crew waited on the flight deck while the aircraft commander and the co-pilot went into the operations center to find out what our particular mission would be. When they returned to the plane, they were accompanied by an Air Force colonel who told us that we would be taking 300 people – mostly children under the age of two from the orphanages in and around Saigon – to Clark AB.

Overwhelmed with my responsibilities for the second time that day, I had no time to hesitate, and the two crews began the task of preparing the aircraft to receive many small charges. The flight crew was an augmented flight crew and those members of the crew who would not be performing actual flying duties on our way back to Clark AB assisted the medical crew. Because of their small size, the children were carried on board in the arms of an attendant and handed from one crew member to another and secured in the seats. The children were secured two to a seat in the troop compartment, and in the case of those in the cargo compartment of the aircraft, they were placed on blankets and secured to the floor with litter straps and cargo tie-down straps. I stood at the foot of the ladder near the aft door of the aircraft and quickly did an "eyeball" assessment of each child as I took them from the arms of the attendant carrying them on board and then handed the child to a crew member to be secured either in a seat in the troop compartment up above or on the floor of the cargo compartment.

What I remember most about enplaning the children is not the sheer magnitude of the process but the pathos of the moment. Many of the children were brought to the plane by young Vietnamese women who were sobbing inconsolably as they handed the children to us, strangers and foreigners from another country, speaking a language they could not comprehend. As I took each child from the arms of each anguished woman, I too wanted to cry. Their pain was palpable and I wished there was some way to ease it and to assure them that I would care for these children with all the tenderness and concern that they had for them. It was with a heavy heart that I took my place along the left side of the aircraft in the lower deck once we had finished loading and were ready for take-off.

An aeromedical evacuation crew is composed of two nurses and three medical technicians. I had split the crew; I remained in the cargo compartment down below with the Charge Medical Technician and had sent the other flight nurse and two medical technicians to the troop compartment in the upper deck. Just moments before we took off, our medical crew was augmented with a medical crew that had arrived on a C-141 shortly after our arrival at Tan Son Nhut AB. I notified the aircraft commander of the additional medical crew and then split that crew so that one complete medical crew was in the troop compartment and the other was in the cargo compartment. The three medical crew members killed in the subsequent crash were all from the medical crew that boarded the C-5 just before take-off.

As we climbed to altitude, one of the adults who was accompanying the children became quite ill. Captain Klinker, Staff Sergeant (SSgt) Paget, and I went to care for her. I do not recall our discussion of what we needed to do, but we did decide to give her some medication. We had stowed the medication kit in the upper deck troop compartment behind the loadmaster's seat in the galley area. I climbed the ladder, knelt on the grate in the floor, retrieved the medication, and was closing the kit and talking to Technical Sergeant (TSgt) Parker, one of the loadmasters, when the rear cargo doors blew open, causing an explosion, and a rapid decompression (RD).

The effects were devastating for us and for the aircraft. It was a classic RD, which is an instantaneous equalization of air pressure, causing anything near the cargo doors to be sucked out of the plane. Once the fog cleared and I could look down through the grate in the floor to the cargo hold below, I saw the South China Sea, a vast, sparkling prism of diamonds as the sun glinted off the water – a sight at once beautiful and horrifying. Moments earlier, the baggage and our medical gear had been secured to the floor of the cargo bay and the pressure wall and cargo doors had been securely fastened. Now they were gone! One medical kit seesawed precariously on the jagged edge of the floor, threatening to fall into the sea below.

I moved from my kneeling position and turned around and looked forward at all the seats where the children were. I saw that SMSgt Howard Perkins, one of the other loadmasters, had followed me up the ladder only to be caught at the gate. He was hanging by his arm, the rest of his body dangling into the void created when the ladder was ripped out by the force of the RD. The oxygen masks were dangling in the air. Crew members donned masks and then proceeded to pull masks to the children, attempting to give each child some puffs of oxygen. We were at 23,000 feet altitude at the time of the RD and lost some altitude quickly. The pilots began a descent to a lower altitude obviating the need for supplemental oxygen. We quickly reviewed the emergency procedures we would use and moved through the troop compartment, re-securing and re-padding all the children and the accompanying adults. Those of us in the troop compartment had no way of getting downstairs to the cargo bay or to the flight deck and had no way of knowing what was happening in other parts of the aircraft. We prepared for a crash landing.

Emergency procedures and safety are fundamental components of any flight training that aircrews and aeromedical crews receive during initial training and flight qualification. While in training, we are drilled on these procedures and how to carry them out until we know them forward, backwards, sideways, upside down, and right side up. This last statement may seem an over-emphasis, but the whole point is that when an emergency occurs in an aircraft, the crew must go into an immediate response of focusing on the emergency and dealing with it. This means that, as a crew member, one must deal with the crisis in an unemotional manner.

The body and psyche's fight or flight mechanism kicks in to the fullest and you may be terrified, but you cannot give in to fear and emotion if you are going to deal effectively and immediately with the crisis at hand. A crew member must learn to thrust the emotion into a side pocket, so to speak, and follow the checklist for emergencies, all the while thinking about how to resolve the problem if following the checklist doesn't work.

That is exactly what the aeromedical crew and aircrew, particularly the pilots, did on 4 April 1975. The ability to do that contributed directly to the survival of so many on board the C-5. Was I afraid when I saw how damaged the aircraft was? Sure, but my flight training had taught me how to deal with both the fear and the need to focus my energies on managing the emergency. It was only after the crisis that I could allow the emotions to have their day.

Our first impact with the ground was like a glancing blow with the rice paddies – bumpy and hard but not any worse than some hard landings that I had experienced on commercial aircraft. However, immediately the plane was airborne again for a few seconds. Then the plane engaged the ground again only this time it was a violent, forceful impact that sent the plane – at least the troop compartment – sailing through the rice paddies like a speed boat, throwing water on the occupants. But it wasn't water, it was mud that slapped and stung us as the plane broke apart. I had been sitting on the floor by the aft row of seats near the galley and ladder area of the aircraft so that I could observe the children. (In Air Force aircraft, the passengers are seated facing the tail of the aircraft rather than forward as is customary in civilian aircraft.)

The violence of the second impact threw me the entire length of the troop compartment. As I was careening down the aisle I could feel the bones in my right foot breaking and other parts of my body banging into and scraping the seats of the aircraft. I remember thinking that it was a good thing that my shoe remained on my foot because I would need to walk on my broken foot during the rescue efforts. Once the plane came to a complete stop, I stood up, and with other members of the flight and medical crew, began to assess the situation.

Stepping outside the troop compartment onto the rice paddies – a feat that would have been impossible in an intact aircraft because the troop compartment is normally six stories above ground – I saw wreckage and debris in every direction that I looked. Running toward us were the members of the flight crew who had exited the flight deck, which was upside down about 100 yards from the troop compartment. Shortly, the Air America and South Vietnamese Air Force helicopters arrived and began to evacuate the survivors to hospitals in Saigon. We carried the children to the helicopters through mud and muck, walking backwards because the rotor wash from the helicopters was blowing debris from the aircraft. SMSgt Perkins, who was the loadmaster who had been ascending the rear ladder to the troop compartment at the time of the RD, used crutches belonging to one of the orphans to splint his own leg so that he could hand children to other crewmembers taking them to the helicopters.

On one of my return trips from the helicopters to the wreckage, I saw a child crawling out of the troop compartment and feared that he would fall into the rice paddies and drown in the mud. As I neared him, I bent slightly and reached down to grab him. When I grabbed him by the seat of his pants, I realized I could not completely straighten up. Holding the child, I walked over to where Major Wallace (one of the navigators on the plane) was standing and asked to be relieved of duty.

I actually have no recollection of doing this, but was told by Major Wallace and other crew members who witnessed it, that I did in fact make such a request. As I approached him with my request, I fainted. When I regained consciousness, he was carrying me and placing me on the floor of a helicopter. Once back at Tan Son Nhut, I was transferred to an ambulance and taken to the Seventh Day Adventist Hospital. The hospital had enacted its triage and disaster plan and cared for most of the injured and set up a morgue to receive the bodies of those who had died in the crash.

After I was assessed and given some initial treatment, I was moved to the courtyard. A short time later, an Air Force flight medical technician came into the courtyard and asked me if I wanted to go home to Clark AB. He told me that some of the survivors of the crash would be going to Clark AB on a C-9 aerovac plane in a few hours. After another ambulance ride through the streets of Saigon, I was back at Tan Son Nhut AB and enplaned on the C-9.

We touched down at Clark AB a few minutes before midnight. The blue runway lights twinkled in the midnight darkness and the plane was greeted by the whole Clark AB family. What I remember most about that landing is the people standing along the fences of the flight line in silent solidarity. Before we were deplaned, General Manor and other senior Air Force officials at Clark AB boarded the aircraft. Last among those to board was Senior Master Sergeant (SMSgt) Andrew "Andy" Smedley, the 10th AES scheduler who was at Clark AB to assist the 9th AES in learning how to schedule C-141 missions. When I saw him, the tight constraints I had placed on my emotions gave way to uncontrollable sobbing.

Suppressing his own emotion, he tried to soothe me and assure me that everything would be okay. He remained with me until the technicians came to get my litter and place me in the ambus (a bus specially equipped to transport litter patients) for the short ride to the hospital. In the space of 12 hours, I had left Clark AB on a C-5 bound for Saigon with an unclear mission other than airlifting people – probably children – from Vietnam, had been involved in the subsequent crash and rescue efforts, had been taken by helicopter and ambulance to the Seventh Day Adventist Hospital, and finally brought back to Clark AB on a C-9 aircraft as a patient.

All of us who returned to Clark AB aboard the C-9 were triaged, assessed, and treated in the Emergency Room and admitted to the Intensive Care Unit (ICU). From the time I started crying when I saw SMSgt Smedley, I continued to cry. I could not stop my tears, and my body was convulsed with uncontrollable shaking. The physician who was assigned to care for me was not only kind but also very understanding in dealing with me. When I said to him that I could stop neither the crying nor the shaking, he said, "You have just been through an extremely traumatic and life-threatening experience. Your crying and shaking are a normal response to an abnormal and horrifying experience." I have often thought of his response and realize how truly helpful it was in dealing with my response to the events surrounding the crash.

As I was lying on the litter in the Emergency Room, the hospital commander and the Chief Nurse, Colonel Louise Marshall, came to see me. It was after midnight, but both of them were dressed in their blue Class A uniforms (what is now called the service dress uniform was actually called the Class A uniform in 1975). I was amazed that they would dress so formally to visit us in the Emergency Room. The chaplains also came. The Catholic chaplain assigned to the hospital came over to me and began talking to me. Although I cannot remember his name, I can still see his face and remember the kindness and gentleness of his manner as he approached me. He asked me if I wanted to pray with him, and when I said yes, he also said, "I have the Blessed Sacrament with me. Would you like to receive Holy Communion?" Answering affirmatively through my tears and chattering teeth, we both prayed together and he gave me the Holy Eucharist. Almost immediately upon receiving the Blessed Sacrament, I stopped shaking and my tears ceased. He came each day to visit me while I was in the hospital bringing the Blessed Sacrament with him. I know that I drew strength from those visits and the prayers that were offered.

Colonel Marshall also visited daily. The visits with Colonel Marshall began a friendship that lasted through the years until her death. When I was later assigned to Hill Air Force Base (AFB) in Utah, I had the opportunity to work under her leadership when she was the Command Nurse of AF Logistics (now Materiel) Command. She was immeasurably helpful to me in dealing with the difficulties of that assignment.

I spent an emotionally wrenching two weeks in the hospital at Clark following the crash. Because of my injuries, I was confined to bed. The crash investigation began immediately and I spent many hours answering questions posed by the investigators and was asked to describe in minute detail everything I could remember of that fateful day. As necessary as the investigations were, they left me with an overwhelming anxiety about the crash and questions always lingered; had I missed something that I should have seen, had I done everything I could have to ensure the safety and well-being of my small charges, had I prepared for the crash landing in the right way?

Myriad questions arose in my mind about what I might have done to change the outcome. Some of the questions that came to mind were irrational, but grief and loss can bring with them a certain irrationality about what is humanly possible in truly overwhelming traumatic events. My heart and soul were drowned in a sea of sadness and loss. My profound sense of loss and overwhelming sense of grief were beyond words and tears, and I could not articulate them to anyone, not even to my husband who so desperately wanted to console and comfort me.

Although I had many visitors from the Clark AB family and received enough flowers to start my own flower shop in my hospital room, I often had long moments of being by myself, particularly after Harriet Goffinett (one of the other surviving flight nurses who was injured in the crash) was discharged from the hospital. I was afraid to let myself fall asleep out of fear that I would relive the experience in my dreams. I am not a person who shares her inner life of thoughts easily or gives expression to feelings and emotions freely; I withdrew into my inner world where it was safe but also very lonely.

I experienced an odd sense of abandonment while surrounded by people who loved me and cared about me. My husband had come to Clark on Emergency Leave, and when he wasn't visiting with me, he helped care for the children that were being brought to Clark on subsequent flights of Operation Babylift. We had been married only eight weeks at the time of the crash and the effect on him was profound. Although his anxieties were different from mine, they were no less real and no less discomforting. It created in him a life-long anxiety about my well-being. Afterwards, whenever we discussed the events of the C-5 crash, we always said that if we could live through and deal with that, there was probably nothing life could throw at us that we couldn't handle.

Once my injuries had healed sufficiently so that I could travel, Bjorn and I returned to Travis on a regularly scheduled aeromedical evacuation mission on 19 April. I was admitted to David Grant Medical Center at Travis and remained there until 21 April when the orthopedic surgeon recommended that I be placed on Convalescent Leave for five weeks. Before leaving Clark, Bjorn had received emergency orders assigning him to Travis and in those days before the internet and online capabilities, the only confirmation anyone had of the orders was a telex message sent between Kadena AB, Clark AB, and Travis AFB.

I am an individual who, like a juggler, must juggle twenty balls at a time or else I become bored. Convalescent Leave was boring and gave me too much time to brood over what had happened. It created enormous anxiety for me. My squadron was particularly stressed and grieving. Of the three medical crew members who died in the crash, two of them were from the 10th AES – SSgt Michael Paget and Capt Mary Klinker. I asked my commander if I could do some duties around the squadron even though I was on convalescent leave. I needed to contribute to the mission in any way I could; our squadron was small, and to have three members missing certainly required the others to work beyond capacity. Operation Babylift, followed immediately by Operation New Life, put tremendous pressure on the squadron in terms of flying. The missions extended beyond the usual Clark to Travis trajectory. Some days, the crews were flying into Travis but then continued on to Florida or Alabama or Georgia or Illinois or Missouri or any of a multitude of points east.

Because I was not able to fly, I started working with the schedulers arranging the many aeromedical evacuation missions and assigning medical crews to these missions. The full effects of the integration of the two squadrons were also having an impact on the squadron; members were beginning to leave for their assignment to Clark or leaving flying altogether for new assignments. Each week, the number of individuals assigned to the squadron decreased but the mission requirements remained the same. The Air Force Reserve associate aeromedical evacuation squadrons – the 40th (now the 446th) at McChord AFB, the 65th (now the 349th) at Travis AFB, the 68th (now defunct) at Norton AFB – that normally flew with us were an integral and significant part of the two operations. Without their full participation, it would have been impossible not only to fly the required missions but also to sustain the non-stop pace of the missions.

By mid-June, the pace of operations and the aeromedical evacuation missions decreased to pre-Operation Babylift levels. The departure of squadron members continued and on 31 August, the acting commander (our commander had already departed for his new assignment) and I locked the doors to the building, signaling the end of the 10th AES and the end of a chapter in the history of aeromedical evacuation. It was another gut-wrenching, heart-breaking day for me. It was as if the dreams and love I had for flying aeromedical evacuation were tossed into the debris of the crash site and swallowed in the mud of the rice paddies as so many broken bodies and twisted wreckage had been on the day of the crash.

In June of 1975, General Paul K. Carlton, the Military Airlift Command's commander-in-chief, presided over ceremonies at Travis AFB and Clark AB honoring the crews of the C-5 for their heroic efforts following the crash. All of the crew members were awarded the Airman's Medal for heroism and voluntary risk of life. In addition, the aircraft commander, Capt Dennis "Bud" Traynor and the co-pilot, Capt Tilford Harp, were awarded the Air Force Cross, the second highest medal awarded by the Air Force. It is awarded for heroism and valor.

In October of 1976, I was awarded the Cheney Award, which is given for an act of valor, extreme fortitude, or self-sacrifice in a humanitarian mission connected with aircraft. The award is named for First Lieutenant William Cheney, who was killed in an aircraft collision over Foggia, Italy in 1918 during the First World War. The award was established by his family in 1927 to honor the memory of airmen who demonstrate heroism under the above-mentioned conditions. I was the first woman to be so honored. I have always felt a sense of embarrassment at being singled out for the award because I believe that the whole crew should have been given the award. It was teamwork and professionalism on the part of all the crew that prevented a greater tragedy. I always have believed that I hold the award in trust for all the members of the crew, living and deceased.

Prior to leaving the 10th AES, I had been told that I would be assigned to the medical center at Travis. Neither the flight surgeon nor the orthopedic surgeon would clear me to fly for at least a year because of the nature of my injuries, so that meant I had to leave flying status. (My injuries included broken bones in my right foot, a compression fracture of the third lumbar vertebra in my spine, a puncture wound to my right leg, and serious lacerations.) My initial assignment to the medical center was to the orthopedic unit; however, my orthopedic injuries and needed recovery time made me ill-suited to work on orthopedics and I was soon transferred to the 2nd Aeromedical Staging Flight (ASF). My understanding of the aeromedical evacuation environment made this an easy transition for me. The staging flights were the facilities that received patients for aeromedical evacuation, prepared them for their flights, ensured that they had all needed medications and supplies, and kept them overnight when there were en route stops before they arrived at their final destinations.

It was while I was assigned to the 2nd ASF that SSgt Phil Wise arrived on a C-141 aeromedical evacuation flight from Clark. Phil had been the Charge Medical Technician on the C-5 the day of the crash. I had assigned Phil to work in the cargo compartment of the plane and that is where he was at the time of the crash. With the exception of three fatalities in the troop compartment, all of the fatalities from the C-5 occurred in the cargo compartment. Miraculously, Phil had survived the crash, although he was critically injured and had spent a significant amount of time recovering from his injuries. He was on his way to Michigan and his home.

My nurse and medical technician colleagues who were working with me that evening freed me from some of my tasks so that Phil and I could have a long chat and visit. It was the first time I had seen him since the crash. We discussed the crash and what had happened to each of us in the now almost one year that had passed since it had happened. We really didn't know each other; Phil was assigned to the 9th AES and I was assigned to the 10th AES. We had only formally met the morning of the crash when he and I were assigned to be part of the medical crew for the mission. I did not see him after the crash. I didn't know what had happened to him and I never saw him while we were patients. This visit in the ASF was the first time we had the opportunity to actually meet each other and discuss an experience we had shared. In some sense, in both the crash and in our brief visit at the ASF, we were like ships passing in the night despite the fact that we had shared a traumatic experience. The next morning, he boarded the aeromedical evacuation mission that took him to Michigan. More than 20 years would pass before I saw him again and really got to know him.

My family was expanding too. I had gotten pregnant in the summer of 1975 and our first child Ellen was born on 29 February 1976. A true leap year day baby, she has always been the subject of good-natured teasing about how old she really is! I worked on one of the medical units at the hospital as the charge nurse after her birth until the summer of 1977. Life had settled into a comfortable routine of work and play. Our second child Diana was born on 16 June 1977. I had been selected for an AFIT scholarship so in August, 1977 I began my graduate studies at the University of California in San Francisco (UCSF) while Bjorn continued to work at David Grant Medical Center. (An AFIT scholarship is one given by the Air Force Institute of Technology to an Air Force member to go to school; all the tuition is paid by the Air Force. It is the member's full-time job.)

★ ★ ★

In many ways I had tried to put the C-5 crash behind me, although it was always present in the back of my mind. There was never a day that I did not think about it, about the children and the others who were on the plane, and most particularly, about my fellow crew members. I called to mind daily the names of the crew members, not in a morbid way but only as a way to never forget them. How could I forget them? I wanted always to remember them.

I was oblivious to the fact that lawsuits regarding the crash were making their way through the judicial system. My first inklings came when I began to receive calls from attorneys soliciting me to join the lawsuits. I was distressed about these calls. They created tremendous anxiety for me because each call forced me to relive the experience all over again. They intruded upon the life I was trying build with my husband and children. One particular call stressed me more than most because I felt as if I were being badgered by the attorney to join the lawsuit. Finally, the attorney became exasperated with me and said, "But we can make some money for you." His comment filled me with horror and disbelief.

At that moment, I felt as though everything that had happened – the crash, the deaths of the children and the adults on the plane, the deaths of the crew members – was reduced to dollars. All the agony and pain of that experience was simply an economic equation that discounted the enormous and overwhelming emotional, psychological, spiritual and physical pain that resulted from the crash, not only for me but for all those who carried the scars of the tragedy in their lives.

Trying to deal with what I had just heard him say, I responded by saying, "Is that what this is all about? Really, is this what this is all about? Making money off a tragedy? I have no plans to make money off a tragedy. There isn't enough money or treasure in the world that can undo what has happened. No amount of money can replace the lives that were lost or the emotional pain that was inflicted on those who survived or on those who were touched by this experience. No amount of money can ever equal the value of one human life. This conversation is over. Do not ever call me again. And tell all your lawyer buddies to quit calling me too. I will have absolutely no part in any lawsuits ever!"

I hung up the phone feeling totally demeaned as a person, that I was just something that could be used to further the ends of the attorneys in their quest of "making money" for their clients. Little did I know that the attorneys' phone calls to me were just the prelude to ten years of emotional struggles and psychological pain that left me feeling totally abandoned. To this day the wounds of those trials are still raw.

Because I had started graduate school at the Catholic University of America while assigned to Andrews AFB and was able to transfer credit for some of my course work, my graduate program at UCSF was only 15 months. Nearing the end of the program and while I was writing my comprehensive exams, I received a phone call from the Air Force telling me that I had to be in Washington, DC, to give a deposition regarding the C-5 crash. Not only did I have to be there, I had to be there the next day! I took the "Red Eye" from San Francisco and flew all night, arriving at National Airport at 8:30 am. I reported to the Justice Department as directed. As so often happened during the course of the trials, it was a case of hurry up and wait. While the attorneys for the plaintiffs, and those of Lockheed, the Justice Department and the Air Force jockeyed with each other over legal technicalities, I sat and waited. I had lunch with one of the Air Force's attorneys and the flight surgeon who had been involved with the accident investigation. After lunch I waited again. At some point in the early afternoon it was decided that I was not going to be needed to give any testimony. I was told I could go home. So, I returned to National Airport and took a 5:00 pm flight back to San Francisco.

This was the typical pattern that developed with the trials. I had to drop everything in my life and go to Washington. The lulls between each trip to Washington gave me a false sense of closure; I tried to continue with my life as normally as possible in between trips. But each call to go again to Washington was like picking a scab and allowing the blood to flow anew. I was tossed back into the horror that was the trials. There were many trips and they all left me feeling as though I were simply a pawn being moved about the chess board to advance whatever ends the attorneys, the plaintiffs, and the courts had in mind at the moment.

Perhaps one such trip can serve as the exemplar of all that was so depersonalizing about the trials. A group of us were waiting in the jury room to testify. Throughout all of the trials, we were not really allowed to see and interact with each other except in discreet ways. The courtroom was like any other court room in the country: tables for the attorneys, the jury box, the court reporter's desk, the judge's bench and the witness chair. The plaintiff's lead attorney was often flamboyant. One particular day, he wore an orange and blue plaid jacket. He was also overly dramatic and definitely accusatory in his questioning, often trying to put words into the mouths of the witnesses.

All of this drama made me feel as if I were in some theater of the absurd, and it only served to increase my anxiety to intolerable levels. When I finished my testimony and left the courtroom, I was told that I could go home (home being Utah at the time). I asked if I could say goodbye to my fellow crew members who were waiting to testify. The answer was a firm no, and I left the courthouse in tears. The inability to say a simple goodbye symbolized to me all the dehumanizing aspects of the trials and was another wound inflicted on my heart. The grueling episode in the courtroom had sapped all my physical and emotional energy and left me totally exhausted. I was so distressed over what had occurred, coupled with my inability to say a simple goodbye to the others, that I decided to take the train back to Utah because I wanted to have nothing to do with planes or anything that reminded me of what I had just experienced. It was an irrational decision but it speaks volumes about my state of mind at that moment.

When I returned to duty at Hill AFB after having been in D.C. for over two weeks, my commander was livid because I had not been there to do my job. Not only did I have to deal with the feelings of being demeaned and devalued by the justice system, I had to deal with the anger of my commander and his lack of understanding of what the experience was for me. He told me I was a worthless officer who neglected her job to go to Washington at the most inconvenient times. Never mind that I had no choice about those trips; I was mandated to go whether I wanted to or not. His attitude compounded the aversion that I had for the trials and only increased my anxiety in trying to do my job despite all the required trips to Washington.

I felt caught between the impossible demands of the Air Force, expecting me to do my job at Hill AFB and requiring me to be a participant in the C-5 trials at the same time. There was no possible way that I could meet those demands. I felt as if my life were careening out of control and there was no way to get it back on course. It was taking a toll on my husband and children as well. My husband had to serve as both parents in dealing with the girls and struggle with his own thoughts and feelings regarding all that was happening. The C-5 experience had been and was a part of our lives from the beginning of our marriage.

I needed to get some control of my life and try to begin to feel like a whole and worthwhile person again. I decided to separate from active duty. The reality is that I did not want to separate from the Air Force, but I saw no other way out of my intolerable situation. I loved the Air Force passionately but I felt abandoned and betrayed by it because of its impossible demands and its failure to understand how traumatizing the C-5 experience continued to be because of the trials. Even today, the only way I can describe what the trials were like for me is to say that they were a form of psychological rape that was inflicted on me against my will. The pain lingers and I still struggle to deal with the trials' effects in my life. The only people who would have come close to understanding what I was experiencing were those crew members who shared the experience with me, but in so many ways, they were off limits to me. The isolation and abandonment were a painful legacy.

In choosing to separate from active duty, I could not completely separate myself from the Air Force. I chose to become a part of the Air Force Reserves as a Mobilization Augmentee and was assigned to the 9019th Squadron in Denver, while my duty location continued to be at Hill AFB as an augmentee to the chief nurse. The day of my actual separation from the active duty Air Force is memorable for what happened when I went to the personnel office to turn in my active duty Identification (ID) card and get my Reserve ID card. The civilian worker who was handling my paperwork looked at me and said, "Are you absolutely sure you want to do this? Because if you don't, I will call Randolph AFB (the location of the Air Force's personnel center) and get it stopped." Overwhelmed with emotion and my conflicted thoughts about separating from active duty, I thought how ironic that a civilian employee of the Air Force who really had no connection to the events of the crash and the trials understood the turmoil I was experiencing better than those with whom I worked. On the verge of tears, I replied, "Yes, I want to separate," because I didn't know what else to say at that point. So, I got my reserve ID card and some paperwork and left feeling very defeated by all that had transpired.

To be once again a civilian was a new and uncomfortable experience for me. My heart ached for the Air Force but I had to pick up the pieces of my life and move forward. Our third child Elizabeth was born a week after my separation from active duty. My original date of separation was to have been several months earlier but I had pleaded with the folks at Randolph AFB to move the date to July. I was trying to postpone my separation as long as possible. I began a doctoral program of study at the University of Utah and also became an instructor in the College of Nursing. Bjorn had separated from the Air Force before I did, when we had decided that only one of us should be in the military because of the responsibilities and demands of parenthood.

The trials still loomed on the horizon, but now that I was no longer active duty, I didn't have to deal with participating in them if I didn't want to do so. And I did not want to participate in them. But I did. Every time I was called and asked to go to Washington, I did. I did not want to let the Air Force down, but more importantly, I did not want to let my fellow crew members down. Even though I felt terribly abandoned by the Air Force, I couldn't abandon my fellow crew members, no matter what the cost. The agony that was the trials really didn't end for me with my separation from active duty.

In June of 1982, after I had completed all my course work for my doctorate, we moved to San Diego and I began teaching at the University of San Diego in the college of nursing while simultaneously working on my doctoral research project. We made new friends, many of them Navy families, and plunged into life in a city that was a Navy town and a resort location. The overwhelming presence of the Navy was a continual reminder of what I had lost when I separated from active duty.

I completed and defended my dissertation in August, 1983, and continued to commute to Hill AFB to do my Reserve duties. I actually did not like being a part of the Reserves because I felt as if I were some sort of civilian-Air Force half-breed, an anomaly that didn't belong fully to either world. I really wanted to be a full-time member of the Air Force. Though I never acknowledged this to anyone or even to myself, that desire was always there floating just below the surface of my consciousness. During one of my periods of anger and frustration with the trials and sadness because I missed the Air Force, I decided to resign my commission and quit the Reserves. I thought doing so would help me to stop straddling civilian and military life. But when I received the letter confirming my resignation, I realized that the finality of my decision to resign my commission solved none of the turmoil I had been living with for all the years following the C-5 crash and the trials. I lay on the floor of my bedroom and cried for hours; my tears were a mixture of sadness, disappointment, frustration, and grief over all that I had lost and all that the C-5 experience and the trials had cost me. At that moment, I did not realize that a major turning point had been reached. It was receiving that letter that started me on the path to return to active duty in the Air Force.

In my faculty position at the university, I worked with the recruiters for the Army, the Navy, and the Air Force who wanted to talk to our students about a military nursing career. I had developed a good working relationship with all three recruiters. One day I asked the Air Force recruiter what I would have to do to return to active duty. At first, he thought I was joking. But after I kept asking him, he finally realized that I was serious and began to help me do what needed to be done to return to active duty. The university, and the college of nursing in particular, had a large representation of active duty Navy nurses in the student body.

One night after a class with the graduate students, one of my students, a Navy Lieutenant Commander, looked at me, and said, "Dr. Aune, you need to go back to active duty in the Air Force. It is clearly where you belong. That is where your heart is and you need to be where your heart is." I was momentarily stunned by her completely unsolicited comment. She had no idea that I had already begun to think and move in that direction. I had discussed my desires only with my husband and the Air Force recruiter. A few weeks later, I told her that I intended to do just that. Of course, all the Navy nurse students found out my intentions so I had my own personal booster club cheering me on for my return to the Air Force!

I was again commissioned and returned to active duty in September, 1986. My first duty assignment upon my return was to David Grant Medical Center at Travis AFB. One of the first things I did when I got to Travis was to drive by my old aeromedical evacuation squadron building. I cried when I drove by the building. I have been back to Travis several times since then and I can never go by the squadron building without crying. Driving by the building is always a bittersweet moment; it symbolizes for me everything that was good and wonderful about my Air Force career and at the same time it reminds me of all that was painful and sad about it. At the same time that I returned to active duty, the C-5 trials came to an end. At last I would be free! No longer a captive of the attorneys, the courts, and the trials, I could embark on my renewed Air Force career with energy and enthusiasm.

I remained at Travis until August, 1989, when I was reassigned to the School of Aerospace Medicine at Brooks AFB in San Antonio, Texas, as an instructor in the Flight Nurse Course. When I returned to active duty I had been commissioned as a captain, the same rank I had when I left active duty. I met the first major's board upon my return and was a major when I was assigned to Brooks. My original peer group of nurses were now lieutenant colonels and some had been promoted to colonel. My new peer group was composed of younger nurses who had entered the Air Force after the C-5 crash.

One day the chair of the Department of Aerospace Nursing and also my boss approached me about sharing my C-5 experience with the flight nurse and medical technician students. In my three years back on active duty, I had shared only once the crash experience. I had been asked to be one of the Flight Nurse Luncheon speakers at the annual meeting of the Aerospace Medical Association the previous May. That speech was a brief five minute presentation that did not focus directly on the crash as much as it focused on what it meant to me to have been a flight nurse. I rarely if ever mentioned my connection to the C-5 crash and never spoke about the trials with any of my colleagues. I was allotted two hours during the last few days of the course to present the C-5 experience. I spoke only about the crash and did it from an academic standpoint, trying to share with the students how the crash experience could be related to what they had learned throughout the course.

Clearly, presenting the experience as an academic lecture set certain parameters but there was also an emotional element to the presentation that could not be avoided. I always allowed the students to ask questions at the end and it was often their questions that evoked the most emotion. One of the recurring questions from the students was whether I had ever met any of the orphans who had been on the C-5. My answer was always, "No." I also added that I had not forgotten them but I had no way of finding them. I had often wondered about them and how they had fared as adoptees. After doing those lectures I was always emotionally and physically exhausted, but I did find that they were a catharsis in dealing with all my thoughts and feelings regarding the crash. My presentations at the school expanded to include the flight surgeons, the aerospace physiologists, and the public health students, though on a less routine basis than with the flight nurse students.

Desert Storm and Desert Shield occurred while I was at the school. On 29 August 1990, a C-5 from the 433rd Reserve unit at San Antonio crashed at Ramstein AB, Germany, killing most of the people on board. Only one of the crew members survived. He was a friend of some of the aerospace physiology faculty. Because he was having great difficulty in dealing with the experience, it had been recommended that he talk about his experience, although he was reluctant to do so. The chief of Aerospace Physiology approached me and asked if I would be willing to meet with this crew member. I agreed and I spent an afternoon recounting what the experience was like for me and he shared his experience and what it meant to him. Although our personal narratives were different, there were commonalities about surviving a major aircraft accident that we could share. Eventually he spoke of his experience to members of the faculty of the school. Before leaving Brooks, I had been made the Chair of the Department of Academics and no longer taught in the Flight Nurse Course, but I did continue to do the C-5 presentation to the students. Each presentation became a way for me to put the experience in perspective.

In June, 1993, I was assigned to the newly founded Graduate School of Nursing at the Uniformed Services University of the Health Sciences (USUHS) in Bethesda, Maryland. Although I was involved with the development of the curriculum for the school and was chair of the Nursing Research department, I did several lectures regarding Operation Babylift, presented at Grand Rounds, and spoke to the medical students about aeromedical evacuation. All of those events were internal to the university, just as all my presentations while in San Antonio were internal to the School of Aerospace Medicine. But, 1995 marked the 20th anniversary of the crash and there was public interest in marking the anniversary. In the space of a few days I was asked to do an interview on C-Span regarding the crash, to participate in the ceremonies at the Vietnam Memorial as one of the Memorial Day speakers, and to do a radio interview regarding the events of 4 April 1975. I had decided to write about the crash and submitted to Military Medicine an article about my experience, which was published in the fall of 1995. I began to feel more comfortable in discussing the experience with a variety of disparate groups.

My four years at the university flew by and in August 1997, I was assigned as the Squadron Commander for the 437th Medical Operations Squadron at Charleston AFB, South Carolina. By this time I had been promoted to Lieutenant Colonel. When I had joined the faculty at USUHS, I also had become a member of the TriService Nursing Research group and spent a great deal of time traveling to various locations with my Navy and Army counterparts fostering nursing research. I remained a member of the TriService group and, even though I was then a squadron commander, I continued to travel on behalf of the group. My days and weeks were filled with all the activities of the squadron, the medical group, and the wing. Our youngest daughter remained in Maryland to finish her last year of high school, and the two older girls were both on their own.

And then I met Aryn!

3

Aryn's Story

When I think of my history and my life, I imagine myself standing at an intersection. Behind me lies a rice paddy, a sea of crops that expands as far as the eye can see. The rice paddy is majestic in its simplicity. Row after row it sways rhythmically with the wind. It is vast, but the details are lacking. No detail, no clear path; it just is.

Directly in front of me is the polar opposite, a cityscape. Everything is tack sharp. I can examine each detail with never-ending depth. The photographer in me focuses on the details. There are cracks in the sidewalk and pot holes in the street, and there are buildings filled with beautiful art. The architecture is detailed and ornate, and within this cityscape are the names, faces and people that have crossed my path.

To understand my past, it is necessary to look back and to navigate to the middle of this vast field and begin to search for details. I stand where the crops reach far and wide, where I have no path, no sense of direction. I can only begin to walk aimlessly in the hope that clarity and direction aren't too far away. More often than not, I stay in the city and never complain. The field lies dormant and continues to sway with a calming peace; it has always been there. No matter how far into the city I travel, the field is always within my sight. Just when I think it doesn't matter, there is always some pull that places me at the edge of the rice paddy again and again, daring me to enter.

Usually, life starts with Mom and Dad and their histories. We learn of our family stories the same way they did. Our parents tell us where they were born, how they met and of all the events that lead to our miraculous arrival into their world. Our lives are just stories we've been told describing the progression of events. It is this foundation that launches us into our lives and prepares us for the lives we will create. Most family histories are neatly packaged with generations of history interspersed with war stories and stories of survival, and filled with curious characters. Usually a few eccentrics are sprinkled throughout, too, that make for great conversation at holiday gatherings.

My past looked nothing like this. There was no packaging at all. It was filled with holes and gaps. There were no characters, no eccentric uncles; there wasn't even a clear date of birth. This was my story, and this was the foundation that would launch me on my path and charge me into the world. While my history wasn't rich in understanding and created more confusion than clarity, I did know a few things. My story was born out of hope, anticipation, war and tragedy. It was built on sacrifice at many levels, so that I could stand before the world and have a chance at life, a chance that would not have been afforded to me without a whole cast of characters who played a variety of roles to afford me a better life than what I would've had in Vietnam.

Each story has a beginning and so does mine. I am Aryn Cristin Lockhart, born in Vietnam with given birth date of July 13, 1974. I was adopted by Americans in April of 1975, and I am the youngest of four children. My adoptive parents had two biological sons and then proceeded to adopt my sister and me. My sister, Cari, and I are both from Vietnam, but are not biological sisters. She was adopted a year before my arrival.

Adoptions were not as prevalent then as they are today. The tides have changed, with multicultural adoptions more common than they were in the '80s. As a child, I knew I was adopted, but it didn't play a huge role in my upbringing. I had much more pressing priorities like playing Wonder Woman with my sister, learning to ride my blue banana-seat bike without annoying training wheels, and having to share a room with my sister, who was always getting me into trouble. We moved to California from New York, and I spent the majority of my elementary school years in San Jose. I liked gymnastics, I loved to read, and it was business as usual in the world of Parkview Elementary. I never gave much thought to my adoption; no one ever asked me about my parents nor seemed to notice I was different. Looking back, I recall there were a lot of Asians in school, but at the time, being a minority was never a single, solitary thought in my mind.

My father worked for IBM, and just before I turned nine, he received a transfer to Manassas, Virginia. I will never forget how my mother prepared us for our move. She would tell us how great it was going to be and how we were going to see snow, lots of trees and have woods where we could play. We'd even have a big yard with trees to climb. The kids were going to be nice and polite because it was the South. "Don't be surprised if they're very gentlemanly, open the door for you or pull out your chair," she'd explain. We had a new adventure before us. My parents were having a home built and we were going to a whole new world. I couldn't wait.

We arrived in Virginia the summer of 1983. Schooling in Virginia wasn't exactly as Mom had described. There were no gentlemanly boys ready to pull my chair out and offer their seats in chivalry. I had been sucked from a simple world filled with childhood innocence and thrust into redneck Virginia – the land of beer koozies, camouflage, and the smell of cows. I would define our neighborhood as upper middle class with custom homes. The parents in the neighborhood were a mix of various business professionals with some active duty and retired military personnel.

Our neighborhood did have trees, as Mom had promised. We did have acres of land where we could play. We were in the DC vicinity, but it had not grown into the metropolitan mecca that it is today. I went to school with a lot of kids whose parents were military or former military. This was my first encounter with anyone associated with the military world. I often found my values were in direct contrast to theirs and even at the ripe, young age of nine, I found myself debating politics with children at the bus stop as we played out the political debates our parents would likely have had.

"Everyone has the right to bear arms," Matt would proclaim.

"That may be true, but I hate guns," I would counter. "I will never understand how it makes sense to counter violence with violence," I would state stubbornly.

"You're a bleeding-heart liberal," he'd say, hurling the words at me as the ultimate insult. "People need guns to protect their families from the bad guys." Smugly, he'd continue, "The only way to protect yourself against a bad guy with a gun is a good guy with a gun."

I would counter angrily, "The answer is not to take up guns, but to educate instead of having a society desensitized to all forms of violence."

The tension would build until we were practically in the throes of a screaming match.

My parents were very vocal about their political views, and as such their views were passed down to me. As a child, I was already beginning to imagine a world where I would make significant impact to do good. My personality was developing steadfast with a headstrong attitude and determination. But like all children, I wanted to be accepted and to have friends at my side.

One unexpected day, I experienced my first scar of prejudice. Tommy Fisher. That fat bastard. I remember him as that big, overgrown, poorly groomed boy in my fourth grade class… overweight, larger than all the other kids, hair dripping with grease. This clearly was not the picture of the Southern gentleman my mother had tried to paint. Dressed in red and black flannel as his staple attire, emanating the smell of sweat and dirt, he lurked in the back of my classroom.

Sitting on the bus, waiting for the other children to make their way and take their seats, I was looking out the window watching as everyone bustled to their destinations. As I sat there, I caught Tommy Fisher glaring into the bus from below. He looked straight into my eyes and opened his grizzly mouth as I heard him chanting and pointing, "Chink, you're a chink." He then brought his hands to his face to create slanted eyes. I wanted to yell at him and throw insults in return, but he was gone before I could react.

The entire way home, I thought about his words. "Why would he say that?" No one had ever dared to call me a chink. I had never even thought much about being Asian and now I was pissed. I went home and immediately told my mother what had happened. As we were talking, tears welled up in my eyes and I said, "I don't understand. Why would he call me a chink?" My mother, direct in her views, was compassionate, as if she had known this day could come. "He's a jerk. Clearly this is not your problem, but his." That sounded like rational logic and yet to a nine year-old, it left me unsatisfied.

Herein lie the teachings of my parents. Neither Mom nor Dad believed I was anything other than their daughter. I may have been adopted, but I was no less a part of our family. My mother believed in raising us in a color blind home. She didn't believe there was any reason to acknowledge or bring attention to the fact that my sister and I were Asian. She often went out of her way to make this point in the face of benign questions. When Cari and I were growing up, my mom was asked by people, "Where are they from?" Her standard answer, "Virginia," knowing full well they were trying to decipher our heritage. Upon further questioning, "No, I mean, where are they *from?*" Again her response is, "Virginia."

I would hate this part of the conversation as I knew clearly what they were trying to ask. My mother was trying to make a clear point. It didn't matter to her; she refused to see any difference, so she expected the world to have the same ability. Neither my sister nor I ever had any knowledge about our Vietnamese heritage. We never learned anything about our culture, the people, or the food. Mom would often say, "You're American. If someone asks where you're from, just tell them America. It doesn't matter where you came from or your race. It only matters that you're a part of the human race," and the conversation would end.

As an adult, I can truly appreciate my mother's philosophies. I can say unequivocally that I never felt anything else except as my mother's daughter. When I looked into the mirror, I never saw Asian, but this would create challenges as I got older. While my mother believed the world should not view us any differently, the truth is, the world is less evolved. The majority of people immediately gravitate to what makes you different. After Tommy Fisher, I saw the difference even if my mother refused to acknowledge it.

Often outspoken, I found myself the target of fights and bullying. Adolescence comes with its own set of challenges. Children can be mean, harsh and unforgiving. I remember many times looking in the mirror thinking if only my eyes were rounder perhaps boys would like me. On the harder days of growing up, I would take my hands to my eyes while gazing upon my reflection and open them widely, wishing my Asian appearance away.

In addition to Tommy Fisher, there were two other significant events that brought my adoption center stage, influencing my perception of self. In many ways I was a late bloomer. I excelled in school, had a studious group of friends, but couldn't get a date to save my life. I buried myself in school, studied hard and prepared myself for my future. In college I began to flourish. I was making friends, finding my unique groups and associations. Dating became a reality, yet I wasn't prepared for what I experienced.

In college I finally began to understand and embrace more of my Asian culture, but it wasn't without challenges. My first boyfriend was in college, a simple, down-to-earth kind of guy. We dated for a couple of years, but as with many relationships, things had run their course and it didn't work out. Before we parted ways, I remember reflecting on the relationship and how things took a turn for the worse.

"I guess I imagined we would have ended up together," I said sadly as we prepared to move on with our lives. "What happened, what went wrong?" In a low voice, he looked at me and said, "We had a great time, but I have to be truly honest with you. I simply did not see myself marrying an Asian." I was speechless. I'm not sure if it's pure irony or torture that my next boyfriend admittedly had an "Asian thing." I had literally moved from one extreme to the other. I went from one who couldn't imagine himself with an Asian to another who had an "Asian thing." Meanwhile, I didn't see myself as Asian or connect with any part of the culture. It was very challenging to grow up in a world where everyone else saw what you could not see. Needless to say, that relationship took a nose dive too.

I had another experience during college that influenced much of my thinking about my adoption and lack of culture. I took the grandiose step to become a part of a sorority. The rituals of sorority life are unique and not fully logical to those outside of the circle. For all intents and purposes, it was a great way to meet, socialize and connect with other women. I went through the obligatory steps to become a part of the Chi Omega chapter at Virginia Tech. My friend, Denise, and I pledged the sorority at the same time.

We were the only two Asians in the sorority, but, of course, I was the last to make that observation. We immediately got along and enjoyed each other's company. We would meet for various sorority events and, while we were friends, we never talked about our heritage or our histories. She was just a friend like any other and it so happened we were both from Vietnam.

One day we were sitting in the sorority kitchen. Our house was positioned on the main street of our college town. Our sorority house had tremendous character, an old Victorian home painted white with its wrap-around porch. One evening as we prepared for an event, Denise and I sat at the kitchen table. In a matter of fact tone, she simply looked at me and said, "Aryn, are you ashamed of being Vietnamese?"

I looked at her puzzled and taken aback, "What do you mean?"

"You never talk about being Asian or Vietnamese, you act like you never have anything to do with it, so I was wondering, are you ashamed?" Denise wasn't known for subtleties. I smiled widely and responded, "No. I'm not ashamed, I just don't have a clue." We went on to talk about my situation and how I had no exposure to or familiarity with my culture. I spoke about my mother's belief of being color blind and how I hadn't even tried Vietnamese food.

Denise's experience was very different from mine. She was a refugee, leaving Vietnam when she was five. Her mother could take only two of her five children to the United States. She was part of the Vietnamese boat people sponsored by her aunt, but also spent time in refugee camps before her family made their way to Richmond, Virginia. She could speak Vietnamese, she understood the culture, she was determined and driven to seek great success based on the opportunities she had been given. We still have a very close bond. She is my expert on all things Vietnamese. The last time we met it was across the world in Prague to share a Vietnamese meal.

These situations played a significant role in how I saw my world. I carried no anger or resentment, nor harbored frustration for my plight in the world. I only remarked upon each of these situations and tried to evolve. These stories were reminders that my life and my circumstances meant that I existed somewhere in between two worlds. I imagined I could be seen as an individual and be judged accordingly, but that wasn't always the case. I learned that the world seeks categorizations. Whether I embraced my own cultural heritage, or had simply not been exposed, the outside world would remark upon my Asian eyes and make assumptions; that was okay.

It was important for my well-being to not take offense and to find some way to embrace how I was different from the world I grew up in. In the same light, I could not fully live within the Vietnamese or Asian culture. On appearance alone, assumptions may be made, but my truth was that I had no real connection to the Asian community. I couldn't relate to the culture, the traditions or the philosophies, and that was okay too. I don't think this is a unique experience for many adoptees. Over the years, I have had the good fortune to meet other adoptees. Some are burdened by the fact that they do not belong fully in either world. I choose to embrace this unique situation with a comfortable acceptance that I fall somewhere in between.

★ ★ ★

This story is 30 years in the making. For as long as I can remember, I was told the story of Operation Babylift and the tragic inaugural flight of the C-5A. My parents kept newspapers, articles, letters, and photos to help reconstruct the fragile pieces of my past. They told me the records had been destroyed on the C-5A, but from all of their clues, I was a part of the initial flight that crashed, leaving 138 dead. While they preserved my tattered sense of history, they also prepared me to accept that what information I could learn of my past was minimal. Sister Ursula, who chose me for my parents, died on the crash and so had any knowledge I could gain of my true origins. My birth date, my name, my circumstances would likely never be known.

My mother would often talk about the turmoil they experienced through my adoption. There were many frantic calls and information voids as they tried to locate my whereabouts after the crash. The entire event was shrouded in chaos and uncertainty. As I was given my history and the stories of my past, the only consistent element appeared to be uncertainty. I would need to accept that I may never find the answers to all of my questions.

The first time I wrote about Operation Babylift and the C-5 was in 4th grade. I entered a creative writing competition and took first place for nonfiction. I had written my brief account complete with hand drawn pictures. Beaming, I received a trophy for my efforts. It was the only trophy I had ever won. It was small in stature, but monumental in meaning. With a small two-inch-square marble base, standing only a mere three inches high, it read, "First place nonfiction." Adorned above the marble base was a cheap, plastic medallion. The gold disc displayed a hand holding a quill poised to write. I treasured that trophy and its meaning. It embodied my love for writing and the story I hoped to tell in its entirety. It served as a gentle reminder to write this story and to tell a thankful tale for all of my blessings.

Writing about Operation Babylift and my association with it has been a lifelong goal, but its scope and focus have evolved. Procrastination, living life, and uncertainty have all played a role in the time it has taken to tell my story. What amazed me was no matter how far away I wandered, there were always signs or people strategically placed throughout my life to bring me back. The pull to write this story has never gone away. "You need to tell this story. Don't wait," was the advice I received. In the end, the time had come for me to wade through the rice paddy and find my path.

4

Discoveries

Aryn:

The college years were the best years of my life. I studied, I partied, I discovered a lot about myself. It was the perfect stepping stone to the never-ending responsibilities that lay ahead as a grown up. After graduating in 1996, it was time to launch myself into the world of career professionals. After working for the government as a co-operative education student for three semesters, I had a smooth transition, starting my government career as a graphic designer in the Northern Virginia area.

After graduation, I shared an apartment with my college friend, Hilary. For the first time, I had the responsibility only of a full time job, where previously I had been juggling several responsibilities to include school, part time work, and various clubs and organizations. I had too much time on my hands. I contemplated graduate school, but the timing seemed right to begin my research on Operation Babylift.

Beside my computer was my notebook, poised and ready as I prepared to embark on my academic undertaking. Initially, I prepared myself to approach my personal history like a college research project. With all my supplies neatly laid out, notebook, pencils, note cards, I sat before my old IBM computer with my dial up connection. The computer made its customary high pitched hissing and dialing sounds before connection. In the Netscape browser, I typed "Operation Babylift." In 1997 the internet was in its infancy. Websites and online information were just beginning to populate the web. As my good fortune would have it, there was an article in the Air Force Magazine about Lt Col Regina Aune.

The article, titled "The Lady was a Tiger," was only a brief synopsis of the events that unfolded on April 4, 1975. I found myself reading faster and faster, getting more and more excited with each word. I had never heard the name Regina Aune from the stories told by my parents. The patchy history my parents offered always included the names and descriptions of those involved with Friends for All Children. There was little if ever a mention of the Air Force personnel.

Much of my history was based on what I could read or discover through various newspapers and articles. These were my only truths. I was mesmerized as I read the harrowing tale and heroic efforts of Regina Aune. After sustaining injuries, she continued to assist carrying babies to the rescue helicopters until she herself lost consciousness. Her valiant efforts resulted in receiving the prestigious Cheney Award.

As I finished the article, a swarm of emotions came over me. I felt a rush of adrenaline, excitement and apprehension simultaneously. I had waited without expectation for the first 22 years of my life. Without knowing about these details of my life, I would still know happiness and sadness, pain and joy. I would still be me, but if I learned about this, could I gain some sense of history? Would it change me?

I was certain Lt Col Aune had answers to questions I had wondered about for years. She would undoubtedly know more about Operation Babylift, the crash, and the details of what happened. I was eager for more facts, images and some clarity to the haze.

I looked to the editor's page and contacted the author, John Frisbee, who gave me Lt Col Aune's information in Washington, D.C. As I scribbled the phone number down and hung up the phone, I ran out to the living room where my roommate was sitting.

"Hil, you won't believe this. I just found the head flight nurse from the C-5 and she's right here in D.C.!" I could hardly contain my excitement.

I rushed back to my room and nervously dialed. The thought crossed my mind, this was all coming together so easily. When I reached the D.C. office, I learned that she had just left within the past few weeks to take command in Charleston, South Carolina. My disappointment was clear, but I knew I was still forging a path of progress.

Over the next couple of weeks, I attempted to call, but without success. I left voicemails, but wasn't able to reach her in person. I was hesitant to leave my life story on voicemail and only indicated I would call back. In the face of these small obstacles, I began to question if perhaps my effortless path had come to an abrupt halt. Just a few days before Christmas, I decided I would try one more time.

Regina:

When I returned from one trip, I had several voice mail messages on my phone from an Aryn Lockhart. I had no idea who Aryn Lockhart was and she never left any information other than her name and that she wanted to get in touch with me. The week before Christmas, I was in my office working on some Officer Performance Reports. I was looking up a word in the dictionary when the phone rang. I answered the phone, and the voice on the other end said, "Hello, Colonel Aune. This is Aryn Lockhart. You don't know me but I was one of the babies on the C-5 Galaxy that crashed during Operation Babylift. I have been looking for you and I just want to say thank you for giving me my life." I was speechless! I had never envisioned meeting any of the children from the flight, although I thought about them frequently. I simply had no idea of how I could find any of them and now at this moment, one of them was talking to me on the phone! I cannot recall to this day what the rest of the conversation was. When Aryn told me that she lived in the Washington, D.C. area, I said that I was going to be in D.C. in February, and we agreed to meet in person.

After hanging up the phone I raced up the stairs to the group commander's office to share with the commander's secretary, Mavis Pearson, my totally unexpected and overwhelming phone call. Mavis had been at Clark at the time of Operation Babylift, and we often talked about that time. She was just as overwhelmed as I was. We decided we needed to talk to Mary Ann Ferguson about the amazing call. Mary Ann had also been at Clark at the time of Operation Babylift and had worked in the 9th AES. She now worked in the 437th Aerospace Medicine Squadron. Our experiences at Clark had bonded us and the three of us had started getting together for lunch periodically when our schedules permitted. Sometimes we reminisced about our Clark days, but more often it was simply to share a friendship. I could not wait to get home that day to share my totally unexpected phone call from Aryn with my husband Bjorn.

Much later that evening, as I was reflecting on the improbable events of the day, I realized that I must have held Aryn in my arms briefly before I passed her to another crew member. As I mentioned earlier, when we were enplaning all the children, I had stood at the bottom of the rear ladder that led to the troop compartment and took each child that was handed to me, quickly did a visual assessment, and then handed the child to the crew member standing nearest to me on the ladder. I was overwhelmed with emotion as I recalled that day and all those children we had put on the plane.

I kept reliving the phone call from earlier in the day hardly able to believe that it had happened. The weeks before we actually met face-to-face in Washington were filled with both excitement and trepidation; I was delighted that I would finally meet one of the "babies!" I relived the events of 4 April 1975 a hundred times a day, and the impending visit filled all my free moments. Bjorn was just as excited whenever we talked about the upcoming visit.

As I reflected on the most unexpected phone call I had ever received, I thought about what a risk Aryn took in calling me. She had no idea how I would respond – with delight or disdain. Needless to say, I was truly overjoyed to receive her call. The risk she took was a risk that was to reap immeasurable rewards, but neither of us was aware at the time that that would be the outcome.

5

Face-to-Face

Aryn:

On a cold February evening, plans were set that Lt Col Aune and I would meet face to face. Our phone conversation was warm and cordial, but that is never the same as meeting in person. I travelled to the Navy Lodge in Bethesda, Maryland. I was a bright-eyed recent graduate, working diligently to forge a path in the world. I believed in the power of first impressions and I felt the weight of wanting to present myself confidently while embodying the hope of those who had set me on this journey from Vietnam.

Once I arrived, I made my way to the lobby where I was greeted by a life-sized anchor. My hands had begun to sweat, and anxious nerves were flowing through me. I stood before the front desk when I recognized Lt Col Aune walking towards me. I recognized her from the pictures I had found online. Dressed in a bright yellow blazer and navy blue slacks, she stood tall and slender before me. Her warm smile greeted me as I offered my outstretched hand and we made our introductions. I was grateful for her kind eyes. I was formal, wanting to appear respectful yet gracious.

We had arranged to have dinner and made the short walk to an upscale French restaurant. As we entered "La Miche," I immediately felt out of place. I looked around to see a variety of middle-aged business professionals who appeared to be unwinding after the work day. The atmosphere was formal, yet warm, with dimmed lighting and candlelit centerpieces. I remarked upon the wooden chairs and the chair rail that adorned the wall. This was not my typical college atmosphere. I was quite certain there would be no rowdy happy hours or dollar pitchers. I welcomed the challenge to adjust to a more professional environment, although I felt I was only playing the part of a grown up.

"We need to order dessert first," Lt Col Aune, told me. "They make an amazing soufflé here, but it's necessary to order it first so it'll be ready for us at the end of our meal."

With a huge smile, I timidly said, "Oh, okay. I've never ordered dessert first." Normally quite outgoing, I was soft-spoken and somewhat shy in my initial interactions. I was anxious for the nerves to dissipate. The dinner progressed and conversation began to take on a life of its own. Soon, I felt much more comfortable. I began to talk about my history and to share stories of my life and family. My nerves had finally calmed and with it our words had a natural flow. We filled the gap of an entire lifetime. We imagined that 22 years prior, I had likely passed through her hands during Operation Babylift on my journey to America.

During our discussions, I learned about Lt Col Aune's three daughters and husband, in addition to some of the highlights of her Air Force career. She was fiercely dedicated to the Air Force and to her family. In the middle of the conversation, my mind would sometimes wander as I continued to marvel at the unique circumstances that had brought our paths together.

After exchanging stories of our lives, I finally gathered the courage to ask about the C-5 crash. I knew there was little likelihood that she could confirm my presence, but this was my first opportunity to get any sense of that day.

"The manifest was lost during the crash," she began. She described how she began the journey in the lower-deck cargo compartment only to head upstairs because a woman was sick. I was mesmerized listening to every word. As she described the accident in greater detail, I did not sense an emotional connection to her words. It was as if she had told this story time and again.

After dinner, we headed back to the Navy Lodge where Lt Col Aune brought her personal scrap books. I sat on the edge of her bed, marveling over the articles and the information that lay before me. These were very different from the articles my parents had saved for me. These articles were less about the tragedy and more about her personal story. They told the story of her early Air Force career and how she had received the prestigious Cheney Award.

In retrospect, the experience of meeting Lt Col Aune was surreal. I could hardly grasp the reality that I met someone who had played a direct role in my history. Uncertainty was the only theme surrounding my past and now I was able to discover more answers. At the very least, I had a clearer picture of that fateful day in April. My mind had already created a vast landscape of imagery based on the sparse newspaper photos I had seen over the years. Now more color and vibrancy had been added.

Regina:

As the holidays flew by and the time drew near for my Temporary Duty (TDY) to Washington, D.C. in early February 1998, I grew more excited and wondered what the moment of our actual face-to-face meeting would be like. I envisioned countless scenarios in my mind as I anticipated our meeting.

I flew from Charleston to D.C. on 28 February and checked into the Navy Lodge in Bethesda, Maryland, eagerly anticipating meeting Aryn and having dinner with her. I planned to take her to La Miche, a lovely French restaurant within walking distance of the Navy Lodge. I had selected La Miche because it was the restaurant where the USUHS nursing faculty always went to celebrate birthdays, anniversaries, graduations, and other momentous occasions. And this was a momentous occasion worthy of celebration! As I waited in the lobby of the Navy Lodge, I kept thinking about the surprising and totally unexpected call in December that brought me to this moment. Despite my excitement regarding our impending meeting, I was also anxious and uncertain about it – not sure how I would respond to actually meeting one of the "babies" face to face.

Aryn arrived at the agreed-upon time. When she walked through the doors, I saw a small young woman who seemed shy and reserved, her round face framed with long dark brown hair, her brown eyes sparkling, her face wreathed in a smile which betokened friendliness and a hesitant but welcoming expectation. I do not remember what we actually said beyond the usual pleasantries of an initial greeting between strangers, but I was overcome with delight at finally meeting one of the babies from Operation Babylift – no longer a baby but a beautiful, poised, and graceful young woman. My initial anxieties evaporated as we walked to La Miche, sharing conversation about ourselves, overcoming the initial awkwardness of a first meeting.

As the evening progressed, we became more at ease with each other. When we returned to the Navy Lodge, I shared some photos and articles regarding Operation Babylift that I had brought with me. The evening seemed to be over before it began, and all too soon we were saying goodbye, but not without agreeing to keep in touch. Thus began a friendship that moved beyond tentative beginnings to an enduring relationship. Neither of us knew at that initial meeting how lasting and deep this new friendship would become, nor how life-changing it would be for both of us.

4 April 1975. The remains of the Galaxy C-5 cockpit after the inaugural Operation Babylift flight crash-landed in the rice fields outside of Saigon's Tan Son Nhut airbase.

photo courtesy of Gerald R. Ford Presidential Museum

Well-worn baby shoes worn by orphans evacuated from Vietnam during Operation Babylift.

1967 Vietnam War Protest reflecting turmoil in the U.S.

Aryn with her siblings.

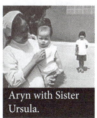
Aryn with Sister Ursula.

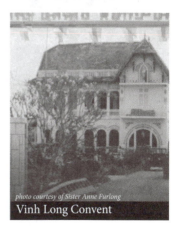
photo courtesy of Sister Anne Furlong
Vinh Long Convent

10th Aeromedical Evacuation Squadron Christmas 1974.

Regina with fellow crewmember SMSgt (Ret) Howard Perkins.

Regina with Col Til Harp, C-5 co-pilot and crewmember Lt Col Keith Malone

CMSgt (Ret) Ray Snedegar with Regina.

Aircraft Commander, Col Bud Traynor with Regina. Several of the surviving crewmembers assembled at Travis Air Force Base in Fairfield, CA to dedicate the memorial for the 22nd MAS members who died on the C-5.

General David C. Jones, Chief of Staff of the Air Force, presents Regina with the Cheney Award October 1976 at the Pentagon.

Regina and Bjorn at her Colonel promotion ceremony.

Lt Gen Rod Bishop officiates over Regina's retirement ceremony October 2006.

Regina's official photo as a colonel from 1999.

Aryn, Diana, Elizabeth, Ellen and Regina

Aryn visiting San Antonio to show her love and support to Diana.

Aryn spending time in San Antonio having breakfast with Bjorn.

Bridesmaids for Elizabeth's wedding.

Aryn visiting the Vietnam Memorial.

Regina and Aryn begin writing Operation Babylift: Mission Accomplished.

Ray, Regina, and Aryn preparing for their return to Vietnam after 40 years.

The crash site as it looks after 40 years, in 2014.

Ray, Aryn, and Regina returning to the crash site.

Here is a shrine located where the rear of the C-5 was found after the crash.

Aryn lights incense on Veteran's Day to honor the C-5 victims.

Operation Babylift 4 April 1975

In loving memory of all those who perished on C5A 80218 on 4 April 1975.

Tưởng nhớ những người đã ra đi trên chuyến bay C5A 80218 ngày 4/4/1975.

Ray, Regina, Martin and Aryn visited a local children's home where many orphans grow up.

The children loved making videos on Ray's ipad and watching themselves.

Aryn's visit to Kajang, Malaysia where she was able to meet the extended family of Sister Ursula Lee including two of her sisters.

Jude Benjamin, Sr. Ursula's nephew, and Aryn meeting in Kajang, Malaysia.

After 40 years, Aryn pays her respects to Sister Ursula Lee who died on the C-5 crash.

6

Adoptee Reunions and Precious Cargo

Regina:

After our initial meeting in Bethesda in February 1998, Aryn and I continued to correspond through emails and infrequent phone calls. Whenever I went to the D.C. area for TDYs (which was fairly often), Aryn and I would always get together one evening of my trip for dinner and "catching up." In fact, our dinners and evenings together were a permanent fixture of my TDYs to Washington. In June, 1999, I was promoted to Colonel and moved from being the 437th Medical Operations Squadron Commander to being the 437th Medical Group Commander, so I did not have as many opportunities to go to D.C., which meant I didn't see Aryn quite as often though we maintained our emails and phone calls. These visits, phone calls, and emails only served to deepen our relationship.

In spring 2000, I received an invitation from the Holt International Children's Services to attend a reunion of first-generation Vietnamese adoptees that was going to be held in Baltimore, Maryland, from 28-30 April at Christ Lutheran Church and Fellowship Hall. When I received the invitation, I told Aryn about the upcoming reunion because I thought she might like to attend, but she was unable to do so because she was going to a friend's wedding.

I drove from Charleston to Baltimore on Friday, 28 April, not sure what to expect or what the reunion would be like. When I arrived at the church fellowship hall, I was overwhelmed by the pictures on display – most of them were of Operation Babylift. Indeed, most, but not all, of the adoptees who attended the reunion had come to the United States during Operation Babylift on either military or civilian aircraft in April, 1975. Seeing these pictures reignited every memory, emotion, thought, and feeling of that April day. I was speechless and somewhat disoriented as I looked at the pictures. Each one served as a vivid reminder of the missions that were Operation Babylift with all of its pathos.

The weekend itself was very structured and had been organized primarily by Holt. However, there were speakers representing not only Holt but also Tessler Adoption Services and The Evan B. Donaldson Adoption Institute, who co-sponsored the weekend with Holt, as well as a representative of the Vietnamese government from the Washington, D.C., embassy. There was free time in between presentations and during and after meals to mingle with the adoptees and their families. Because I was in my Air Force uniform, I stood out in the group and was approached by many adoptees and their families with questions they had regarding Operation Babylift. I also met several adoptees who had been on the ill-fated flight on 4 April 1975. Those meetings, though few, were emotional, both for the adoptees and for me. Those free times and mini-discussions were a wonderful opportunity for me to get to know the adoptees in a more personal and individual way. The stories they shared touched my heart and filled me with many new memories to treasure.

The reunion was structured so that the agencies that operated orphanages in Vietnam during the war, the adoptive parents, and the adoptees themselves each had time to present their stories from their various perspectives. The presentations were interesting, but even more, they revealed just how chaotic, difficult and uncertain the last days were for the orphanages in trying to get the children to their adoptive parents before South Vietnam collapsed, and how equally chaotic and uncertain it was for the parents in knowing whether, when, and where they would receive their adopted children. The adoptees' stories in particular were deeply personal and touching, as well as truly reflective of the unique and individual personalities of each of the adoptees. The poignancy of their individual narratives was punctuated often by tears and frequently by self-deprecating humor. One could glean a real sense of what it was like, not only to be adopted, but also because of the nature of their adoptions to have no history save the history that was created for them through their adoptions.

What also struck me about the adoptees' presentations both individually and collectively was the gratitude each one expressed over the life that was now theirs because of their adoption. Not all their stories were happy ones with Cinderella endings, but they were all underscored by a profound sense of gratitude toward their birth mothers, their adoptive parents (who, as many of them highlighted, were their "real" parents), and the country that they now called home. It occurred to me as they spoke that, in addition to the ethnic differences of being Asian and mixed-race adoptees, the offspring of a war-torn country, they faced many other issues, including the insecurities of adoptees in general, who wonder about their origins, their birth families, and the why of their adoptions.

As I listened to their stories, I thought back to my fellow crew members from the C-5 and all the crews and people who worked so hard in Operation Babylift, and I wished that they could be sharing the moment with me. Surely, the tragedy of that day and the subsequent Operation Babylift missions created an unbreakable bond between the "babies" and the crews and people who worked so hard to get them to safety, even if they never personally knew each other.

The weekend ended with a bus trip on Sunday to the Vietnam Memorial in Washington, D.C., for a closing ceremony and the laying of a wreath and flowers at the Wall followed by a farewell brunch at the fellowship hall back in Baltimore. It was both an emotionally exhausting yet an exhilarating time for everyone.

Prior to the weekend in Baltimore, I had received a phone call from Janet Gardner of the Gardner Documentary Group around the same time that I received the invitation from Holt to attend the reunion. Janet Gardner was planning to do a documentary on some of the Vietnamese adoptees, their stories, and a trip back to Vietnam, and she wanted me to participate in it. She had arranged to be at Dover AFB in Delaware the same weekend as the adoptee reunion.

After leaving the reunion, I traveled to Dover AFB to meet Ms. Gardner, her film crew, Col Bud Traynor, and Aryn, who was returning from her friend's wedding and made a detour through Delaware to participate in the interview. We all met at the main gate at Dover AFB Sunday afternoon - Bud Traynor, Aryn, Janet Gardner and her crew, the Dover AFB Public Affairs (PA) folks, and I. After the customary introductions, the PA staff took us to a C-5B parked on the flight line to do the interview. While Bud and I were certainly at ease around the aircraft and with flight line protocol and activities, it was a totally different experience for Aryn. I sensed that she was overwhelmed by the whole situation. It was not only her first meeting with Bud, it was also the first time she ever saw a C-5 aircraft. Although Bud and I could speak to the sequence of events of 4 April 1975 and to some extent approach the interview in a more technical and detached way, that was not true for Aryn. On one level it was not true for me either. Because of the bond we had forged, I think I keyed into all the emotion and feeling that Aryn was experiencing as she took in the enormity of what had occurred on that April day in 1975. By the time the interview was finished, we were both emotionally drained. I know that after having spent the greater part of the weekend at the adoptee reunion, I was physically and emotionally exhausted and very glad that I was spending the night in quarters at Dover AFB.

Aryn:

In 2000, I learned Col Aune had received an invitation to an adoptee reunion in Maryland. I was living in the D.C. area, but already had a prior commitment in New York and was unable to attend the reunion.

I quietly wondered how the reunion experience would affect Col Aune. We had begun to build the foundation of our friendship with periodic visits, emails and phone calls. I had been the first adoptee to locate Col Aune and I selfishly wondered if she would create new or better bonds with other adoptees or survivors of the C-5 tragedy. I simply had to wait and see.

Col Aune was asked to participate in a documentary about Operation Babylift that same weekend. The maker of the documentary, titled "Precious Cargo," wanted to interview both Col Aune and the pilot, Col Bud Traynor (ret.) for their film. As she described her extensive travel itinerary, she was hopeful I could find a way to meet her in Dover, Delaware, saying, "If you can meet me, I can arrange for you to have a private tour of a C-5."

I did not want to let the opportunity pass me by. I began to imagine that I could actually stand in a C-5, I could sit in the troop compartment and understand its complex layout. I could take the images I had fabricated in my mind and replace them with actual pictures. I could understand the structure of the plane and imagine the intensity and chaos of April 4th. Perhaps, I could gain a better understanding of what had happened during the accident. I could not miss this.

Traveling over 400 miles and eight hours, I drove from Buffalo, New York to Dover. My body was worn and exhausted, but my mind was intensely alert. I did not want to miss a single moment. Upon my arrival, I met Col Aune and together she stood with the pilot, Bud Traynor. I was mesmerized. Not only was I getting a private tour of a C-5, I was also meeting the pilot. I felt unprepared, overwhelmed and nervous. As I extended my hand, I had no words to capture my feelings. I could only hope he could feel some of my heartfelt gratitude.

Lacking eloquence, I offered only the simplest words. "Thank you. It is such an honor and I am truly grateful." I hoped he could feel the tiniest fraction of the intense emotions brewing within me.

We were escorted to the flight line, passing a row of C-5s. The aircraft were a dull, light gray. They lacked any character or personality. I had flown commercially throughout my life, but these planes were twice their size. I had seen pictures of the C-5, but it could not prepare me for the sheer magnitude of these monstrosities. There was a steep metal ladder that led to the cargo portion of the aircraft. We climbed to the top on a shaky ladder, which brought us to the vast cargo bay.

The cargo area was dark and cavernous. Our voices and footsteps reverberated off the cold, metal walls. The C-5 was designed to transport large military equipment and vehicles such as tanks, helicopters, and Humvees. It was difficult to imagine the bay littered with babies and adults covering the entire floor. The cries of children and chatter of adults shuffling and preparing for departure would have echoed throughout this cave. Along both sides of the cargo bay were narrow benches used as walking paths to move to the front and back of the aircraft when the cargo compartment was full. On April 4th, these narrow benches were used as additional seating for the children.

We walked through the dark cargo compartment towards the back of the plane. The only light shone from where we had entered. As we headed towards the rear cargo door, I tried to take in every detail. Nothing but cold metal surrounded us on all sides. The air was damp and cool, reminiscent of a basement. When we arrived at the rear cargo door, I just stared. There is a large ramp that lowers to allow the large equipment to be loaded. Enclosing this ramp are two cargo doors. These doors and their malfunction cost 138 people their lives. I listened as Col Bud Traynor pointed at the locking mechanisms that had caused the crash.

Traynor explained, "The locking mechanism hinged across the pressure door failed because they weren't properly rigged. The ramp dropped, ripped off, and then the door suddenly went straight back into the tail of the airplane." He went on to show me how the locking mechanisms were close to the hydraulic lines. When the door blew off, it severed the lines, making it impossible for him to maneuver the plane. Without the heroic efforts and quick thinking of both the pilot and co-pilot, it is certain there would have been more fatalities.

I toured the entire aircraft from head to toe. I sat in the cockpit and the troop compartment. I was able to ask every question I could recall. Climbing the narrow and unstable stairwell to the troop compartment, I listened as Col Aune described the human chain that had brought the smallest cargo upstairs. The troop compartment seats faced the rear of the plane. The seats appeared dated and looked very different from commercial airlines. Col Aune explained how the arm rests were taken out from between the seats and two babies were placed together. I wondered, had I sat in seats like this 25 years before?

By the end of the day, I was emotionally and physically exhausted. No longer were images fabricated in my mind. I stood in that enormous cavity imagining an entire scene around me… echoes of children crying, confusion and sweltering heat. I sat in the troop compartment with the clear image of babies squished to fit as many as possible into the seats. In my mind, history – my history – had come to life.

★ ★ ★

An article in the *Washington Post* by Shaaren Pine titled, "Please don't tell me I was lucky to be adopted," was written by a woman adopted from India as a young girl by Caucasians. She described some of her own struggles as an adoptee. I've learned we all have a cup of suffering. It is unhealthy and unwise to compare our world to that of others, and yet we always seem to find a way.

I was surprised by the statistics she offered. Based on a 2001 study of adopted adults, adoptees were 2.5 times more likely to attempt suicide. Additionally, she cited that adoptees were twice as likely to receive counseling in addition to experiencing a much higher rate of substance abuse. I had spent a lifetime suffering through my own over-thinking, but I never correlated my struggles to being an adoptee. I thought it was just my character to overanalyze and work through identity challenges.

Before the ease of social media and connecting as adults, most of us existed in isolation through our adolescence. We are all connected by our parentless origins and we have processed and experienced our lives differently. The question is this: Does this make us any different from those who know their history and their parents?

I do not wish to cast my opinion upon other adoptees and their experiences, but I am interested in our stories. Portions of her article resonate with me. I can relate to feeling a lack of connection to my heritage, to wishing myself white and the heavy burden of feeling indebted. Just by circumstances alone, there was a persistent reminder of strangers playing an integral role in my ability to live my life. People honestly mean well when they say, "Your mother must have loved you so much that she gave you away." In our case, there is little recourse for these words. We can only offer a silent smile and nod that perhaps they know something we do not.

At one point in my life, I was encouraged to thank Vietnam veterans for my life. It is difficult to describe the heavy burden bestowed upon me and the feeling of indebtedness to complete strangers. I felt like society required me to express gratitude to anyone involved with Vietnam. Though I had no awareness of the intensity of war or the horrific circumstances the war created, I was led to believe that every soldier of the war played some role in my ability to live, as they were fighting for "my people."

These sentences frequently made me cringe: "If not for Vietnam veterans fighting for your people, you would not be here." "If not for the nuns in the orphanages, you would not be here." The truth is, most people do not have the heavy shadow cast upon them with the reminder, "If not for……" While I have always felt a sense of gratitude for my circumstances, these statements always left me with tremendous feelings of guilt.

At times I did walk up to Vietnam vets and thank them. It was awkward and difficult. I knew many vets made sacrifices during their service, but as time went on, I saved my words for those directly associated with my story. Vietnam vets lived through a harrowing time during some of the darkest hours of our country's history. Soldiers were vilified, and often they did not receive the emotional support they needed upon their return. I am now at peace, recognizing that, while I am a product of the Vietnam War, I am not responsible for the vets nor for their experiences.

From a holistic perspective, I can appreciate their sacrifices. I have visited the Vietnam Memorial and each time it has left me solemn with a heavy heart. Within the vast sea of names and the lives lost so tragically, I feel an indescribable connection. The memorial is divided into years. Under 1975, my hands have traced over the names of the C-5 crew.

Feeling the cool granite beneath my fingers, I passed over the etched names, remarking how the C-5 crew members were some of the last casualties of the war.

★ ★ ★

The first time I met other adoptees was at a reunion in 2000. Because of Operation Babylift, the majority of us were close in age. Most of us were in our mid 20's and discovering who we were, and the reunion inevitably seemed to lead us to one another. The year 2000 was the 25th anniversary of Operation Babylift, and interest in the adoptees had been rekindled.

I was living in New Mexico and was fortunate enough to learn about a reunion occurring just a few hours away in Colorado. It was organized by Friends for All Children, the organization my parents worked with for both my sister's and my own adoption. I had already begun my research, and had met two surviving crewmembers, Lt Col Aune and the pilot, Bud Traynor. I had even received a private tour of the C-5.

In the beautiful Rocky Mountains, I made my way to the YMCA camp in Estes Park, Colorado. I was full of nervousness and apprehension. What would the other adoptees be like? Would I belong?

Upon my arrival many adoptees were in small groups with their families, making preliminary introductions. Normally outgoing, I found myself shy and reserved, observing more than participating.

Despite my reservation, an adoptee came my way. "Hi, I'm Chris," said a young Asian guy, offering his hand to me. Like all of us, he had no accent and beyond his appearance, I sensed nothing traditionally Asian about him. A tall, blond woman offered her hand from behind Chris. "This is my sister, Julie," he said nonchalantly.

For an instant, I was a taken aback. I felt like a light bulb went off. I get it now. I grew up in a home where my parents and my brothers were Caucasian. I didn't think anything of it until others brought it to my attention. I lived with my brother during my second year of college and there was this frequent assumption that we were married. As with any sibling relationship, my first reaction was, "Eww." Blind to my own circumstances, I just accepted that people did not fully understand how my brother and I could look so different, and went about my world. It was not until this moment that I got it. As I extended my hand and graciously received Julie's handshake, I thought, "Okay. Now I see. It actually looks unusual." Chris, small in stature with his dark hair and almond shaped eyes, next to his taller, blond haired, blue-eyed sister was quite contrasting. What I previously could not see in my own family, I saw in parallel with Chris and Julie.

Despite my initial hesitation, there was undoubtedly a sense of connection amongst the adoptees. We were given an opportunity to have a closed-door session where only the adoptees could talk amongst ourselves. For many of us, it was a sense of true belonging where we were not the excluded, as we had felt throughout our lives, but we found a community within ourselves. We shared our experiences together and were shocked to hear how similar they were regardless of where we had grown up or what our unique upbringing entailed. Many felt as if we had found long-lost brothers and sisters. Several of the adoptees were meeting again after an initial reunion in April of the same year. Plans were made to continue building our unique community.

Based on my experience, I have created my own categorization of adoptees. There are those of us who are grateful for our circumstances and who recognize the significance of our adoption. There are some of us who carry a heavy burden and a sense of emptiness, always seeking and searching for answers with a hope and desire to connect to something biological. I have met adoptees who are angry and resentful of their circumstances, particularly if their adoption experience was negative, but not necessarily because of that. I have met others who are completely ambivalent. My sister and I were both adopted, and while it allowed us a commonality as children, as adults it became insignificant. My sister is ambivalent about the adoptee process. She has no desire to meet other adoptees, return to our homeland, or identify with the Vietnamese culture at all. This is her choice, but it is vastly different from my own.

I will always hold the experience of that reunion close to me. It was the first time I had been exposed to so many adoptees in one, central location. I am still connected with some I met there. The reunion experience was overwhelming. It felt very paradoxical. Growing up, our similar circumstances made us stand out: our lives are affected by looking different from our parents and siblings, and our origins were often filled with questions and unclear facts.

The reunion was essentially a gathering of strangers, all with the single, common thread of being Vietnamese adoptees. As with all social gatherings, cliques formed and those who were similar gravitated towards one another. On one hand, I felt like I was part of a unique and elite group, and yet on the other hand, I felt a sense of isolation. After years of reflection, I feel that it resembled a high school reunion. I was never in the most popular cliques, but I was always on the periphery with connections to a variety of groups. Despite our common connection, I struggled to feel included. I think there was often an expectation that the moment we came together, we would feel like a hole had been filled as we shared similar experiences. I believe this happened for some adoptees, but it did not for me.

Because of this experience, I chose to travel to Vietnam as an individual and not as part of an adoptee group. Furthermore, I have not attended any other reunions, yet I am glad reunions continue to occur. I do stay in touch online and enjoy following my fellow adoptees through social media. I am forever linked with my adoptee community; however, I have made the choice to create my connections one at a time.

7

Together in New Mexico

Regina:

Aryn and I continued our sporadic meetings when I was TDY to Washington throughout the rest of 2000 and into 2001. My job as commander for the medical group at Charleston kept me busy, so most of our communication was through emails and phone calls.

In late spring of 2001, Aryn told me she was moving to Albuquerque. My two years as group commander would come to an end in early summer, and I was anxiously waiting to learn what my next assignment would be and where it would take me. Once again I had been selected for the commanders' list and was hoping that I would get another command. (Commanders are selected from a commander-eligible list. Everyone on that list is selected by a board that determines who among the eligible colonels are "commander material," so to speak. Commanders can be chosen only from this list.)

Several weeks after Aryn told me about her impending move to Albuquerque, I received notification that I had been selected to be the commander of the 377th Medical Group at Kirtland AFB in Albuquerque and be moving there in late August. How fortuitous! I could not wait to tell Aryn! Now we would be in the same city and would definitely have more opportunity to see each other.

My new location also meant that Aryn could finally meet Bjorn. All our meetings and visits had taken place in Washington, and since Bjorn did not accompany me on my TDYs he had gotten to know Aryn only vicariously through my recounting of our visits and sharing the experiences with him. He had wanted to meet Aryn but simply had not had the opportunity. Because she was part of our history due to the Operation Babylift experience, she already had a special place in his heart – a special place that was to grow exponentially over the next few years, particularly as he got to spend time with her and really got to know her.

We moved to Albuquerque in late August. The first week was spent doing all the necessary "in-processing" and getting settled into our house on the base. The change-of-command was scheduled for September 5th outdoors on the grounds of the VA Hospital. The 377th Medical Group was a joint venture with the VA, and the clinic building was located on the VA grounds and not on Kirtland AFB.

I had invited Aryn to the ceremony; in fact, I had listed her among the individuals who were to sit in the VIP section with my family. She had become such a part of my life that it was only natural that she share in the ceremony. The ceremony was followed by an outdoor reception, but later that evening I had a reception at my home for family and friends. I had, and still have, several cousins who live in Albuquerque and they came that evening. My good friend Theresa Casey, who was the medical group commander at Langley AFB in Virginia, had come to the ceremony, as well as Phil Wise, one of the crew members. The gathering at my home was not large, but it was a lovely evening and Aryn had the opportunity to meet my family and friends. Unfortunately, Ellen, Diana, and Elizabeth could not be there so Aryn did not get to meet them.

September 5th was a Wednesday, and on Thursday and Friday I continued my in-processing so that Monday, September 10th, was my first real day in my office as the commander. I always say somewhat facitiously that it was my only normal day at Kirtland because the next day was September 11th and the events of that day were unfolding as the duty day began. I will never forget that day. Because Albuquerque is on Mountain Time, the events on the East Coast were happening as most residents of Albuquerque were heading to work and to school.

I had barely gotten to my office when one of my squadron commanders came rushing into my office to tell me that a plane had hit one of the Twin Towers in New York. No sooner had she told me that than my secretary told me that the Command Post was calling me. The message was to report to the headquarters building immediately. Because the clinic was co-located with the VA Hospital and off the Air Force base, I had to travel one mile to get to the Gibson Gate to enter the base, and then once on the base travel another mile to the headquarters building. I just made it through the gate before it was secured and no one could get on or off the installation. When I got to the briefing, the full impact of what was happening as we were being briefed began to sink in. My days were definitely not normal for several months. I never left the base from September 11th until late November or early December, other than a few occasions when I left it to go to my office in the clinic. I had to manage the clinic from the Battlestaff in the headquarters building.

Needless to say, even though Aryn and I were now living in the same city, we still did not get to see much of each other in those chaotic early months following September 11th. But we did talk frequently on the phone.

When Elizabeth came home from college in early December for Christmas, she and Aryn finally got to meet. They established a friendship immediately, and from then on whenever Elizabeth was home from school they got together. That first Christmas we spent in Albuquerque, Aryn was able to meet Ellen and Diana when they came to celebrate the holiday. She not only met the girls but also Diana's husband Erick and the grandchildren, Kirsten, Makayla, and Anthone. So, now Aryn was fully incorporated into what my daughters call our "crazy Aune household."

Although there continued to be tight security at Kirtland, as 2001 became 2002, I did not need to stay in the Battlestaff as long or as frequently, and had in fact been able to work from my office in the clinic. This also meant that I had more freedom to leave the base. Some sense of normalcy began to prevail in everyday life despite the continued heightened alert posture. Aryn and I were able to see each other more often, have coffee together, and dinners at home or at restaurants. Bjorn became a regular part of these gatherings. His relationship with Aryn grew. The year marched by and we celebrated important days such as Easter, Mothers' Day, Fathers' Day and the holidays together. In May 2002, Aryn married her fiancé, Gary. Aryn also got to meet and know my mother, because she visited us several times in 2001 and 2002.

Elizabeth came home from college for summer break in early May, and she and Aryn spent time together when they weren't working. I actually think they spent more time together than Aryn and I did during the summer months. In late August, we had a farewell party for Elizabeth when she left for England for her study abroad program. Bjorn and I ended 2002 with a trip to England to see Elizabeth and to spend Christmas with our friends Paula and Jerry Rabon and their family, who were assigned to Mildenhall AB, not far from where Elizabeth was going to school. She frequently spent weekends with them while she was in England.

The year 2003 quickly approached and with it the realization that my tenure as medical group commander at Kirtland would be finished in early summer, and I would once again have a new assignment and a move to a new location. In May 2003, Elizabeth graduated from college just five weeks before Bjorn and I left for San Antonio and my new assignment as the 59th Medical Operations Group Commander at the 59th Medical Wing (Wilford Hall Medical Center) at Lackland AFB. We had a graduation party for Elizabeth, which also was a farewell for us.

Aryn and I had a scant 22 months living in the same city, and though we crammed as much time together as we could, it seemed as though we'd had only a few days together. But, by the time of my farewell dinner, Aryn certainly knew she was part of the Aune family. The day we left Albuquerque for San Antonio, Aryn came to bid us goodbye.

Aryn:

The military is filled with formalities and traditions; the proper way of addressing an officer is one of these. Always wanting to offer the appropriate respect, I chose to deliberately refer to Regina Aune by her official rank. When I met Lt Col Aune, she held the rank of Lieutenant Colonel. While stationed in South Carolina, she was promoted to Colonel. The spoken greeting remained the same so I continued to refer to her as Colonel Aune.

By now it had become a regular occurrence that when Col Aune was in town, we would meet for dinner. It had already been three years since our initial contact and meeting. After our shared experience in Dover with the Precious Cargo documentary, there was little awkwardness and we had fallen into the comfortable familiarity of two friends catching up. It was during this last meeting in 2001 that I informed Col Aune that I was moving to Albuquerque, New Mexico to be with my fiancé. We had met two years prior and spent the past year apart. I had decided it was time for me to make the move.

Within a few short weeks after meeting Col Aune in DC, I received a phone call. "Hi Aryn, it's Regina." She never referred to herself as Col Aune. It was my formality and it became a term of endearment as much as it was a form of respect.

"You won't believe this," she started. I listened curiously. "We're moving to Albuquerque too. We'll both be stationed at Kirtland."

How amazing! In this huge world, we would find ourselves in the same city on the same base. Coincidence seemed to be on our side. I looked forward to getting more opportunities to catch up and to finally meet the family I had heard so much about.

Col Aune arrived in Albuquerque in September of 2001. The first order of business was her change of command. I received an invitation, but was unprepared for its formality and the number of Airmen she would be commanding. Despite working in the D.C. area, I did not have a true understanding of rank and the responsibilities associated with rank structure. I worked at a headquarters command where ranks are often inflated. I would have Colonels conferring with me to organize retirement programs for Generals. A rank of Colonel at headquarters may lead a small program, whereas at a smaller base, a Colonel may oversee hundreds of soldiers or airmen and make critical decisions affecting the entire base.

When I arrived for the change of command, I was not prepared for the fanfare of the ceremony I was about to witness. On a warm, fall day, there were hundreds of fold-out chairs set up and scores of people beginning to filter to their seats. As I made my way to the general audience seats, I held my camera close and observed. I watched the impressive ceremony in a sea of Air Force blue, as command flags were exchanged, salutes were exchanged and the hundreds of Airmen accepted their newest commanding officer. After the ceremony, I met with Col Aune, who introduced me to her husband for the first time.

"Aryn, this is my husband, Bjorn." I shook his extended hand. With a kind smile he warmly greeted me, letting me know he had heard a lot about me. It was during this introduction that I glanced into the VIP section and saw my name on the back of a chair. I had no idea I was supposed to be a VIP, nor did I have any idea what it meant to be a commander. This woman, with whom I had casually shared meals, had tremendous responsibility for hundreds of Airmen. She was their leader and it gave me a different perspective of the significant responsibilities associated with being a Commander.

As I made small talk with Col Aune, a man with a cane and a slight limp walked towards us. I could see a light peppering of grey in his hair as he approached. Together, he and Col Aune exchanged a warm, welcoming hug.

"Aryn, you must meet this man," Col Aune stated with great importance. "This is Phil Wise. He is another surviving crew member and one of only a few who survived from the cargo compartment."

It was impossible to hide my surprise. I looked at this man and warmly shook his hand. I had now met a third surviving crew member from that fateful day. We chatted politely as I learned he had travelled from Michigan to attend the change of command. We shared only a brief exchange, but it was here that I learned of the severe injuries he sustained from the crash. We never spoke in great detail about his experience, but it was clear the events of that day had changed his course in life.

Col Aune's arrival and her introduction to Kirtland were quickly hastened by the events of 9/11, a few short days after her change of command. With her busy schedule, it was some time before we were able to spend time together.

While in Albuquerque, I met Col Aune's youngest daughter, Elizabeth. She was home visiting from college. We made plans to meet at a local coffee shop, and hours later we were both amazed at the ease of conversation. We chatted casually about life and school, and a little about how I had come to meet her mother. As the early evening turned to night, we had quickly become two friends catching up, sharing laughs and stories.

We were invited for dinner around Christmas, where I learned her entire family would be in attendance. I had met Col Aune's husband, but this was the first time I was going to meet all three of her daughters. I wasn't quite sure what to expect. We were quickly greeted by the bustling noise of children's voices and adult chatter. The house was full with three daughters, a son in law, and three grandchildren.

Elizabeth and I had already had our introduction, but Diana, Ellen and I were meeting for the first time. The atmosphere of this first meeting was polite, but cautious. I sensed the greatest reservation from Diana, the middle daughter. She had recently broken her elbow; her arm was incapacitated in a cast and sling. She was polite, but I didn't particularly get a strong sense of warmth or welcoming. Diana was a young mother and it was clear she was in charge as she projected a strong sense of authority. As the night progressed, we found ourselves in the kitchen while the rest of the family was gathered towards the living area. In no uncertain terms, she simply looked to me and without hesitation said, "What do you want?" I looked at her completely taken aback. I wasn't prepared for such an outright, blunt question. I knew immediately what she was trying to imply and didn't attempt to appear naive.

Without any defensiveness, I simply stated, "I don't want anything. I promise, I am not here with any intentions." I felt her continuing to assess me and recognized immediately she was protective of her mother and would ensure anyone with ill intentions would be warned. I understood her concerns, but instead of feeling put off or creating walls between us, I admired this direct approach. I was not trying to overstate my position nor assume an important role in Col Aune's life. I was simply grateful for her warmth and the opportunity to have a small tie to my past.

By our next meeting, Diana and I had created a genuine bond. She quickly saw I was true to my word and had no expectations. I did, however, manage to give her the nickname "Spade." I respected her no-nonsense approach. Over the years, I would come to depend on her directness. She was always willing to call a spade a spade.

★ ★ ★

Over the two years Col Aune spent in Albuquerque, our relationship progressed. With the advantage of proximity, we were able to see each other more frequently sharing dinners, holidays and special events. Time moved quickly and after two short years Col Aune and Bjorn were moving to their next duty assignment in San Antonio, Texas.

We made plans to meet for dinner before their departure. I was sad to see their time in Albuquerque end. Our relationship had evolved as I was fortunate enough to meet the entire family and create my own relationships with each of them. The years were quickly passing, and I was grateful that our paths had placed us in the exact same town and base for this period of time.

Dinner conversation consisted of reminiscing over the past few years in Albuquerque and promises and plans to visit San Antonio. Toward the end of our meal, the conversation took a twist.

"Aryn, we need to talk," Bjorn looked at me sternly. I stiffened slightly trying to anticipate his words. "The time has come. You have to stop calling Regina, 'Col Aune'."

I looked at him blankly. Slowly a grin came across my face. Bjorn was always very happy and jovial. He never interacted with me sternly. I look at him inquisitively.

"I know I have continued to be very formal," I began, "But my usage of 'Col Aune' is as much a term of endearment as it is respect." I had been very deliberate in my choice over the years to use 'Col Aune.' In the beginning, it was important to be respectful and over time, its connotation evolved to something unique for me. There was only one Colonel in my life and she held a very unique place in my past and in my present. It was my intention to be formal to the rest of the world, knowing there was greater meaning below the surface.

"What should I call the two of you, then?" I asked, unsure whether I could transition to a first-name basis.

With his wide, familiar smile and his blue eyes gazing upon me, he responded, "How about 'Mom and Dad'?" Together, they talked about how I was no longer just an adoptee they'd met, but I had become a part of the family. They were sincere in their words and I knew too our lives were no longer on two paths, but had merged to one. There was tremendous love and respect between us.

My eyes widened. I wasn't expecting that. I began to stammer, "Uhh, wow. That's huge."

This was a big deal for me. Growing up, I had parents who took titles very seriously. The only people who received the appropriate title of Aunt or Uncle, Grandma and Grandpa were those who had that direct connection. While we shared other very close relationships that were family-like, they still did not use family titles or adjectives.

It is not the same in all families. There are families where close friends become "Aunt" or "Uncle" and it's simply second nature and comfortable. This was not my case. Perhaps because I was adopted or because of how my parents saw the importance of titles, to use Mom and Dad was no small request. Family was not defined by who shared our lineage, but the titles were reserved. There was great importance that I was my adopted mother's daughter and she my mother. This meant no matter what happened in life these facts could not change. She would always be my mother and I, her daughter. In that split second, I could not say with confidence that I could call Col Aune and Bjorn, "Mom and Dad."

I struggled with this request more than others might have. I was so touched they wanted me to call them Mom and Dad, and yet, I was torn with my own interpretation of the words. I worried about disrespecting my adopted mother and father. I believed in the significance of words and the power they hold. It was a long process of acceptance. I was finally able to find the perfect title that allowed me to accept their request, yet still create some separation. From the time they moved to San Antonio, the Aunes became my SA Mom and Dad.

8

Deployed

Regina:

The year 2003 quickly turned into 2004. Aryn remained in New Mexico and continued working at Kirtland AFB while she pursued a Master's Degree. In June 2004, I was notified that I was scheduled to deploy to Kuwait as the Medical Group Commander at Ali Al Salem AB. Preparing for a deployment is a tedious process. In addition to doing any readiness training, gathering all the required gear and clothing, getting all the mandated immunizations and medical clearances, and attending briefings, there is a requirement to ensure that all one's personal affairs are in order. This requirement includes the execution of a will.

While executing a will may sound frightening, it is a fact of life for military members. From the moment a military member takes the Oath of Office or the Oath of Enlistment, the member is, or should be, aware that the ultimate sacrifice may be demanded of him or her at a moment's notice. Most of us in the military realize that what is unstated in the oath is a willingness to give our lives in the defense of the nation whether in combat or non-combat operations if that is required. I certainly not only knew that but also realized how quickly and unexpectedly that could happen, because of my experience in Operation Babylift – a non-combat humanitarian operation.

When Bjorn and I discussed what I was going to put in my will, it was already a foregone conclusion that Aryn would be a part of it. Knowing the why and the what of executing the will, I did it in a straight-forward and matter-of-fact manner and really thought nothing more about it. I know that it made our daughters uneasy; they did not view it so unemotionally. Aryn did not know beforehand that she was named in the will, so when she received her copy of it, she was both shocked and surprised that I had included her.

Aryn:

After New Mexico, my SA Mom and Dad moved to Texas for their final duty station when SA Mom received news of deployment to Kuwait. At the time, Kuwait was a more welcome option than Iraq, but still a location of concern.

I received a message indicating I'd be receiving some mail in the coming days. I took note, but thought little of it as she often thoughtfully sent a card or gift when she thought of me. I remember vividly the moment her mail arrived this time. I had just returned from work, picked up the mail, and walked into the door of my house.

As I opened the mail, I noticed it was a stack of papers. As I pulled it from the envelope, it read "Last Will and Testament."

I read its content, thinking it unusual that she would send this to me. I continued to read and my eyes widened in shock. Right there in black and white – right there on a legal document – in the case of her death, "I hereby leave..." I saw my name in and amongst the names of her daughters.

My immediate thought was Diana. It hadn't been that long since I had felt her threatening glance upon me. Almost in a panic, I called her.

"Uh, Diana, I just got something in the mail," I said anxiously. "I just got Mom's will and testament. Have you seen this?" Diana calmly responded, "Yes, I have a copy, too. What's wrong?"

I'm thinking, "What's, wrong? Are you kidding me?" Just a few years prior, Diana had specifically asked what my intentions were. I was adamant that I had none and here I was on the same line with Mom's daughters. This felt concerning.

"I just wanted to get your thoughts on what was in the will," I said cautiously. She and I had an appreciation for directness.

Without missing a beat, she replied, "It wasn't just talk, Aryn. When she said you were part of the family, she meant it." Diana continued teasingly, "It's completely fine. We have all accepted that you're part of the family. This was Mom's call and we all support it, so you can get over it now."

Over these many years, I have heard those words more than a few times from Diana. "Stop calling yourself an outsider. You're part of this family; get over it." Despite the repetitive assertions of familial acceptance, I struggled with this concept.

I never felt anything but accepted into the Aune family, and yet I have always respected there is some separation between this family and the adopted family in which I grew up. I did not grow up with these girls. I am not tied to them except by our choice, and for that reason I have always felt a respectful caution. I offered opinions diplomatically or cautiously, though I often second-guessed the contribution. As the years wore on, my guard lowered, and I was always amazed at the openness and willingness of the entire Aune family to embrace me.

When you are intimately intertwined into a family it means you accept all parts of it; you inherit the good, the bad, and the periodic drama. From the point our paths crossed, our lives began the gradual union where we no longer travelled separately. Through time, space and commitment to each other, our paths merged. We became bonded by the events and experiences that many families share – weddings, births, celebrations and, sadly, my divorce, as well as family sickness and death.

It was within these years, SA Mom and I began talking about writing a book. It had always been my lifelong dream to write, and the relationship that was unfolding seemed the perfect closure to a story long forgotten. Operation Babylift completed its last mission on April 26, 1975, evacuating approximately 3,300 children. The military mission was completed because of the fall of Saigon, but its true completion came as we adoptees continued in our lives. In the relationship that was forged with my SA Mom, we had come full circle.

Regina:

In September 2004, I deployed to Kuwait and was there until late January 2005. Our fourth grandchild Amiyah was born in October 2004. Although I missed her birth as well as Thanksgiving, Christmas, and my birthday with my family and missed being with them, I found my deployment experience rewarding in unexpected ways. Bjorn was not alone for Thanksgiving; he went to Albuquerque to spend it with Aryn. Elizabeth had been working in Boston following her graduation from college, but in December she returned to San Antonio and began working for Methodist Hospital on the Bone Marrow Transplant Unit.

The night in January when I returned from my deployment, Bjorn, Elizabeth, my deputy commander, and other members of my 59th Medical Operations Group greeted me at the San Antonio Airport – a sacrifice of sleep for them since I returned to San Antonio at 1:30 am! I was overjoyed to see them, but I was exhausted. My trip home took nearly 48 hours. I flew from Kuwait City to Aviano AB, Italy, to Rhein Main AB, Germany, to Baltimore, to Atlanta, and then finally to San Antonio. There were plane changes in Baltimore and Atlanta, and each place on the itinerary involved at least a two-hour stop. I was so happy to be home and see my family, and they were so happy to see me, that despite my exhaustion we opened a bottle of champagne and stayed up until 6 am talking and enjoying being together again.

While I was in Kuwait, the girls planned a 30th wedding anniversary party for us. Our actual anniversary date was 8 February but they planned it for late February to ensure that I was home from my deployment. Aryn not only was involved in the planning, but also came from Albuquerque to share in the festivities. She continued to be more and more integrated into the daily and usual activities of Aune family life.

In late spring, Aryn graduated from her Master's program and wanted all of us to be there. So, all of us went to Albuquerque to celebrate with her. The graduates each chose two people to hood them, and Aryn asked Elizabeth and me to do her hooding. The Master of Ceremonies not only announced the graduates' names and degrees, but also who was doing the hooding for each graduate. I was momentarily surprised when the Master of Ceremonies announced Elizabeth's and my name and said that we were her sister and her mother respectively. At that moment, I thought how far our relationship had come from a simple telephone call the week before Christmas in 1997!

When I returned from my deployment, I spent a few months at the 59th Medical Operations Group, but it was time once again to move on to another assignment. This time, I did not have to leave San Antonio. I moved from Lackland AFB to Brooks City-Base and to the School of Aerospace Medicine as the Chairman of the International Expeditionary Education and Training Department, which was composed of five divisions, all involved with some aspect of international medicine. It was to be my last Air Force assignment, because my mandatory retirement date was 31 December 2006.

Aryn continued working in Albuquerque, but in late 2005, she was presented with the opportunity to take a graphics designer position at the Marshall Center in Garmisch-Partenkirchen, Germany. She was uncertain about taking the position. We discussed it in terms of both its pros and cons and the advantages of taking an overseas assignment. She decided to take the position and make the move to Germany. She came to San Antonio just after Christmas to see all of us. By that time, Diana, Erick and the children had moved from California to San Antonio when Erick separated from active duty with the Army.

We had a wonderful visit and wished her well in her new job. Unbeknownst to her, we had gone to the Build-A-Bear store and had a teddy bear made with recordings of the children's voices telling her that they loved Auntie Aryn, and sent it to Germany so that it would be there when she arrived. We had put other things in the box too, so that she would have some things to remind her that we all loved her and were going to miss her. In early February 2006, Aryn left for Germany and her new adventures. She found a nice apartment and settled into her new job and new surroundings. Once again, we maintained contact by emails and phone.

9

Celebrations and Revelations

Regina:

While Aryn was settling into life in Germany, my Air Force career was winding down and I began to think about my retirement. I had accrued 90 days of leave, and since I intended to use all my leave before I retired rather than "sell" it back, I planned my retirement for early October. I wanted General Robert "Rod" Bishop to officiate the ceremony. He had been the wing commander at Charleston and had selected me for my first group commander job. Logistically that was a challenge because he was the Commander of 3rd Air Force and stationed at Ramstein AB, Germany at the time. The date moved several times before it was finally fixed for Friday, 6 October in the evening. I also asked Chaplain, Father Robert Bruno to do the invocation and the closing prayer at the ceremony. He was then assigned to the Pentagon in Washington and had to make sure his schedule was clear – another logistical challenge! I had the ceremony combined with a dinner at the Kelly Club, with music provided by the jazz ensemble of the Air Force Band of the West.

Although I had made up the guest list with those I wanted invited in addition to those required by protocol, I did not know who was coming because the individuals in charge of the arrangements password protected the RSVP list! I was happily surprised by how many people from across the years of my Air Force career were there to celebrate with me and had wanted to surprise me; hence the reason the list was password-protected. Aryn came from Germany, bringing with her Matthias Martin, whom she had begun dating a short time after she arrived in Germany. I was happy that she was a part of the festivities. Our fifth grandchild, Erykah, had arrived on 28 September, so she was eight days old when she "participated" in my retirement!

Ray Snedegar, one of the C-5 loadmasters from the Babylift mission, attended the ceremony so he and Aryn had the opportunity to meet each other. She had already met Phil Wise at my change-of-command ceremony at Kirtland in 2001 and Bud Traynor at Dover for the Precious Cargo interview in 2000. Now she was able to meet another crew member involved with Operation Babylift. The day after my retirement ceremony I had an open house at my home for all the out-of-town guests, and then it seemed like it was suddenly Sunday and everyone was leaving to return to their homes. Aryn left too after an all too short visit.

In December, Bjorn and I flew to Italy to spend Christmas with the Rabons, who were now assigned to Aviano AB. The four of us flew to Rome for Christmas, attended Christmas Midnight Mass at St. Peter's, and on the Tuesday after Christmas attended Pope Benedict's Papal Audience before flying back to Aviano AB and then home to San Antonio on 2 January.

On our return to San Antonio, I "traded" my active duty ID card for my retiree ID card and began a new job. Thus, 2007 began quietly. With 5,559 miles between us, Aryn and I communicated by emails and phone calls as we always had when we were separated by distance. She and Martin (although his name is Matthias he goes by Martin) surprised us with an unexpected visit in spring. It was a treat for all of us and we had a delightful visit that was over all too soon. The year slipped by quickly and it was Christmas again.

Aryn:

During 2006 my life took some significant twists and turns. In what seemed a blink of an eye, I changed jobs, I changed countries, and most of my life seemed unrecognizable to me. I went through the painful process of a divorce and wanted nothing more than a fresh start. That start came in the form of a new job across the ocean in Germany, working for the American government.

I was anxious for new beginnings and it didn't get more extreme than leaving everything I knew and starting over. I always had a form of impulsiveness within me. Because of my history, I would often think,

"Why not? I've been given the amazing opportunity to make choices; why not challenge myself with taking the risk?" I would assess my circumstances, assess my risks and, frequently, leap. Sometimes that leap propelled me forward into great possibilities and sometimes that leap left me battered and bruised. No matter the outcome, it seemed sooner or later, I'd do it all over again, not always choosing the safe or secure path.

While I missed certain parts of living stateside, I came to truly appreciate the German culture and its people. Germany is full of rules, with discipline and order being at the forefront, and yet culturally they live more in the present. As an American, I always felt like I was chasing the ultimate dream. I was convinced that through hard work or luck, I could have it all – the money, the power, the influence. Living overseas taught me to slow down. I was still fiercely driven, but I never tired of seeing the world from a different perspective. I travelled throughout Europe, allowing myself to appreciate the varied cultures and traditions. The hardest trade-off for the experiences was the distance from family and friends.

Despite oceans between us, life continued to move forward and so too did my connection with the Aune family. I was integrally woven into the family. I became the accepted entity. I travelled back to the states for SA Mom's retirement. It was the Air Force that allowed our paths to cross, and her connection to the Air Force was forged with great love and dedication to her service. This was a monumental moment for her, and I was honored to share it with her daughters, her husband, and her closest friends and family.

SA Mom was extremely busy during the events and I socialized with the sisters and met the newest member of the family. Diana had given birth to Erykah just eight days prior. The next day, SA Mom had a small reception at the house for some of her out-of-town guests. I was mingling in the kitchen when mom walked up with a tall grey-haired gentleman.

"Hi, I'm Ray," the man said, extending his hand. I had never seen him before.

"Aryn, this man is very important. This is Ray Snedegar. He was the loadmaster who survived the C-5 crash too," SA Mom explained.

I was speechless. I was in my own world and jolted to attention. I had no idea I would meet another crew member at this event. I quickly counted up all of the connections I had made because of SA Mom. I had found her almost 10 years prior, I'd met Phil Wise, one of the few survivors of the cargo compartment, I had met the pilot, Bud Traynor, and now Ray Snedegar, the loadmaster.

Ray was joined by his wife and we chatted for some time. He was very friendly with no air of pretension. I felt like I was catching up with a buddy over a beer.

As I maneuvered through the challenges of overseas living, it seemed no matter how frequently I moved away from the book, something always brought me back. If people learned of my story, they were immediately intrigued – conversations started and interest was generated. In one situation, my work colleague asked me about the progress of my book every time our paths crossed. He played an integral role in gently prodding, always reminding me time and again, "No one else can tell your story. So start. Now."

When I would make my way back to my research and back to my story, I felt like I was starting from the beginning. I hoped with each word, each connection, each email, the story was building and soon it would lie neatly before me. As I blew the dust off of my notebooks, it was time to dive in – again.

Through my research, I learned Vietnamese adoptees came from a handful of agencies that were working during the war. Friends for All Children (FFAC) was the organization with which my parents worked for both my sister's and my adoption. FFAC was led by Rosemary Taylor, an Australian. Her organization grew to four nurseries throughout Vietnam facilitating the adoption of thousands and spanning the years from 1967 to 1975.

The efforts of Rosemary Taylor, in addition to her staff, seem incomprehensible to me. She single-handedly took on the plight of orphaned children. She forged a path sending us worldwide in the hopes of allowing us a better opportunity than what was available to us in Vietnam. She endured the painful loss of children dying around her, and yet she still maneuvered through corrupt bureaucracy at the height of war, placing hope and encouragement within each of us. She shrank the globe, sending children throughout the world to places ranging from America to Australia. Rosemary Taylor had developed a complex operation managing an international staff of Australians, Americans, Germans and local Vietnamese women.

While Rosemary Taylor has served as somewhat of an idol for us, she detests being placed on any form of pedestal. She dedicated her entire life to orphans and children like me, though she has no interest in the spotlight or to be seen as any form of saint. This was her contribution to the world, and for me she is an amazing example of the goodness of people and the power of choices.

The earliest stories from my parents told of Friends for All Children and of Sister Ursula. Sister Ursula was in charge of the nursery at my orphanage located in Vinh Long. The convent where I spent my early days did not fall under Rosemary Taylor and Friends for All Children, yet the organization worked closely with many orphanages throughout the countryside, helping us to find homes worldwide.

I was always grateful for the aging newspapers and hand-written letters my parents kept for me as souvenirs of my earliest days. My family album is a pile of letters written on fragile, thin paper to facilitate international mailing. Sister Ursula was one character who took center stage in my parents' stories. She chose me to go to the Lockhart home. The paperwork ready for approval had the name Phung thi Thanh Phung, Sister Ursula's first choice for my parents. I learned from her letters that she had changed her mind several times before finally settling upon me. Once her final decision had been made, I would travel on the first baby's paperwork. During those times of chaos and uncertainty, paperwork was a necessary drill and it was not always done to the letter following all the rules strictly. The nuns, Rosemary Taylor, and her staff, did everything within their power to pass the required obstacle and get us out of country. Birth dates were just numbers and names were simply a formality.

Sister Ursula was the keeper of these untold stories. She had left her family in Malaysia to serve and dedicate her life to the church, which led her to children like me. She had been in Vietnam since 1960 and was asked to be a last-minute escort for Operation Babylift. She happily accepted, and within a few short hours it had been determined she would be returning to her beloved Malaysia for good. In the saddest turn of events, she died in the C-5 crash.

My adoptive mother always ensured I knew the importance of Sister Ursula in my life. Without her, I could not have my amazing life. Throughout my life, she has always been with me, guiding me with love.

As children, we adjusted to our families and focused on the day-to-day moments. As we grew into adults, the questions began to surface. What could we possibly know of our pasts? Would we find any answers to understand our origins?

For Friends for All Children, the majority of our answers came from one person, Sister Susan McDonald. She had taken on the responsibility of sharing whatever information was available, and she gave that information freely, yet the information was still sparse at best. As I began to search for more answers, she was my first stop.

I found a handful of books that offered a glimpse into the war during that time. I began to collect pieces and parts of information like a squirrel gathering nuts. A few books talked about Operation Babylift, and each time, I read them looking for more clues. I later learned of books written by Rosemary Taylor in addition to a small book written by the nuns from my orphanage. I am beyond words and appreciative that they took the time to write their memoirs, giving me a glimpse of my origins. When I sought some clarification to one of the books, I contacted Sister Susan. Over the years she had frequently been contacted by adoptees looking for any crumb of information. It was in this email, my world stopped.

As I inquired about some facts from a book I had recently read, Sister Susan offered the information she had regarding me.

"Your nursery name was Yvonne at To Am and you left on the Pan Am plane April 5, 1975. I see you were from Vinh Long and that your birth certificate came from Vinh Long, with your name Phung thi Thanh Phung born July 13, 1974. You came to Saigon from Vinh Long on March 26, 1975, so most of your days were spent in Vinh Long. Either the sisters brought you to us, or perhaps we went to Vinh Long to get you and others during the heat of the last days."

The information in black and white stared at me. I silently looked upon the words questioningly. My entire history has been relegated to a few short sentences. April 5? Was she saying I was not in the crash? I had built my life's history on my parents' belief that I was on the flight. My mother's only caveat had been that because of Sister Ursula's death, it was possible I may never know the full circumstances of my arrival. In years full of clouds and unclear information, this seemed so matter of fact. Black and white – no uncertainty. Bam!

To this point, I had started my research, I had forged a close relationship with Regina Aune, I'd had a personal tour of the C-5, I had met crew members, and I was gathering information to write a book, and now, in one simple sentence, I was not part of it?

With no desire to appear melodramatic, this was a tremendous blow. Can one person, now, after all of these years, be so clear and so certain?

The only way I had heard anyone describe the C-5 events and that time was with chaos and uncertainty. I felt like my legs had been cut out from underneath me. I felt like a fraud. So much of how I had created my identity was based upon the belief that I had survived the crash.

We continued to corresponded more as I tried to uncover more facts. While I was still in a state of disbelief, there was little I could do to argue a point or fathom another possibility. This is the simple state of our lives. When tattered scraps of our history do exist, they are passed down from people who were often loosely connected to our circumstances. These were her facts, and I had no evidence to refute her information. I simply had to accept her words, and wonder.

After receiving these emails, I made two phone calls – one to my adopted mom and one to my SA Mom. When I spoke to my mother, she remained adamant about the facts that affected their conclusion.

"You were Sister Ursula's last, best baby. She would not have left without you," my mother stated matter-of-factly. She went on to explain, "Not only that, upon your arrival we had you checked out immediately by the doctor. He was very clear about the fact that your ear drums had burst and healed over. The ear drums bursting would have been a result of a rapid decompression." With that, the topic was complete.

My phone call to SA Mom took a very different tone. Since our initial contact, my nerves had long dissipated and our conversations had since taken on a comfortable familiarity. This one was one of those moments where the nerves came back. I wasn't exactly sure what I should say or how it should be said.

"I just received an email and I'm not sure how to react," I started tentatively. "I just need to know, would it matter if I was not on the C-5 flight?" With those words, tears began to flow. I continued, "I searched for you because this had always been my belief, but now I am not sure about anything. I feel like I need to apologize to you, and yet I know there is no way I could have known anything differently." I paused through my shaky voice, "There are still so many unanswered questions, and now I am afraid to find out what else I will uncover." With nothing but kindness and compassion, SA Mom replied, "Aryn, it is okay. There is a good likelihood that we may never know exactly who was on that flight." Reassuringly, I could feel her empathy towards me, "It does not matter. What you told me changes nothing!"

I felt relieved for her reassurance and yet, I struggled. These were my facts. These were the stories I had been told and had accepted as my history. Based on these beliefs, I had set a path, and now the foundation was crumbling beneath me. Inside I felt like a fraud; though a fraud is one who deliberately sets out to deceive, and I had not, I still felt a heavy weight had landed upon me.

My mother still believes fully that I was a part of the inaugural flight, and SA Mom describes chaotic circumstances and the well-known fact that the manifest on the flight was lost in the crash. To add additional uncertainty, I learned that surviving children from the crash also departed on 5 April 75 on the next Operation Babylift flight. It is possible I left on the 5th and could still have been a part of the inaugural flight. What is left for me? In my mind there continues to be nothing but uncertainty. I know only that I always have a moment of hesitation when telling my story. I speak with less confidence and never say with certainty that I was or was not part of the crash. I only say I have always believed that I was a part of the crash.

As the years went on, I came to learn that I was not the only one in this circumstance. Many other adoptees believed they were part of this tragic event, only to be told conflicting information years later. As we were then forced to find or reevaluate our histories and identities, I began to ask myself, does it matter? It matters that there were so many lives lost on that tragic day. It matters to me that Sister Ursula was on that flight, and there is nothing that can refute that she cared for me and chose me for my parents. Now, 40 years later, I am here living this life. Does it matter if I was there or not? I do not know.

I am still in charge of the choices of my life. Operation Babylift and the inaugural flight still play a significant role for me and affect my personal identity, but I would be a liar if I were to say that I don't feel confused and conflicted at times. Real doubt has been placed on my path, and I cannot stand as tall or as confidently when I speak of my role.

I did not let this debilitate me or my goals. I continued to research my past, I continued to learn about Vietnam, Operation Babylift and the C-5 crash. I continued to dream of the day I would write my book and return to Vietnam.

Regina:

Aryn's narrative account of her communication with Susan McDonald and her extreme distress at finding out that she wasn't on the C-5 is a more benign response than mine was when she told me what Susan McDonald had told her. I remember well the day Aryn told me that

Susan McDonald had informed her that she was potentially not on the tragic flight, and therefore not involved in the crash. I was deeply distressed, but I was also angry.

Aryn's anguish and distress seemed to overwhelm her as what scant knowledge she had of her origins and her history were so ruthlessly torn from her. She apologized to me and told me that she felt that she was a fraud. She certainly had no reason to apologize to me and she most definitely was not a fraud. Aryn feared that this wholly unanticipated revelation would destroy our relationship. I ached for her anguish, but I also tried to reassure her that, whether she was or was not on the C-5 did not and would not change anything. The relationship that developed following our first telephone encounter was certainly strong enough to weather this small storm and was not dependent upon whether or not she was on the plane.

Later, as I reflected on what she had told me and recalled both the day of the crash and the day she and I spent going through all her documents, meager though they were, several thoughts emerged, and I shared them with her. The chaos of that day in April 1975 is almost too difficult to comprehend, even if you were an eye witness to it as I was. Because we lost all the documents related to the babies, there is absolutely no way anyone can know or claim to know with any certainty which babies were actually on board the aircraft. Although there were some older children on board who could talk (and they all perished in the crash), most of the orphans were babies who could neither talk nor walk.

From that day in Albuquerque when Aryn and I went through her documents, we both knew that she was substituted for the baby whose paperwork she traveled on. So, although her paperwork says she is Phung thi Thanh Phung, she is not. In a handwritten letter from Sister Ursula to Aryn's adoptive parents, Sister stated that she had chosen another baby for the Lockharts but would use Phung thi Thanh Phung's paperwork. Sister Ursula was on the C-5; I remember having a brief and light-hearted conversation with her before we took off. I will always remember it because she was so happy and joyful and anxious for the babies to get to their adoptive families.

Sister Ursula subsequently died in the crash. It would seem to me that, if she had personally chosen Aryn, she would have had her with her on that fateful flight. Aryn grew up believing that she had been there, because her parents told her that was what had happened to her. Why would any parents tell their child that she had been in a horrific crash if it were not so? Loving parents do not make up horrific stories to tell their children at some later date. I believe that Aryn was on the C-5, despite one individual's comments to the contrary.

Aryn is not the only adoptee who was told this. I have heard from other Operation Babylift adoptees who had been told and believed all their lives that they were crash survivors only to be told by Susan McDonald that they weren't. As Aryn did, several have apologized to me for taking up my time by asking questions regarding that day and the crash. Some have shared Aryn's feelings of being a fraud. I have tried to reassure them that they are not frauds despite what they might feel, and that they have nothing for which to apologize. Whether or not they were on the flight, they were part of Operation Babylift and they are survivors. I am disheartened that so many adoptees have been told in what appears to me to be a heartless and cold manner that they were not on the plane and therefore could not be crash survivors.

I reiterate what I said previously: given the extreme chaos of that day, no one can say with any measure of certainty which babies were or were not on the plane. But beyond that, these adoptees have been told by their parents that they were survivors of the crash. To deny that is, in effect, to call their parents liars or at least call into question their integrity. As distressing as it was for me to have Aryn, and then others, tell me that they had been told that they were not on the C-5 when they have believed for their whole lives that they were, I cannot begin to fathom the depth of anguish it caused and continues to cause them. To have their origins clouded by such uncertainty, especially after they have believed a particular narrative all their lives, can lead only to tentativeness and hesitancy on their part in discussing aspects of their origins.

In terms of Aryn and me, nothing has changed in our relationship – other than that it has grown deeper and even more meaningful and important in our lives. No matter how many times I tell Aryn that I believe she was on the plane, she displays a hesitancy and a tentativeness whenever she speaks about Operation Babylift or her origins. Such tentativeness is due to her doubts about her belief regarding how she got to America. It creates a definite self-consciousness in her regarding her beginnings, and she exhibits a certain discomfort whenever she talks about it. And every time I see it, I get angry. I am angry not only for her and the doubt that was seeded in her psyche regarding her Operation Babylift experience, but also for all the others who were told from childhood that they too were survivors, only to have that small piece of their understanding of their history shredded before their eyes by a single comment of one individual.

10

Storms Upon Us

Regina:

In late December 2007, our daughter Diana was diagnosed with an aggressive form of breast cancer. Erykah, the baby, was only 15 months old and Diana had turned 30 that previous June. It was a shock to all of us, especially because both the surgeon and the oncologist said she had no risk factors for developing cancer other than being a female. She had surgery several days after New Year's Day in 2008 and began chemotherapy on Valentine's Day. Before going to her first chemotherapy treatment, she and I went to Aldo's Restaurant to have lunch. Forgetting that the restaurants would be extremely busy because it was 14 February, we arrived at the restaurant to find that there was no table available. But, the host, sensing our disappointment, quickly arranged a table in front of the fireplace so that we could have lunch. It was a special moment for both of us as we prepared to navigate uncharted waters as Diana began cancer treatment.

Bjorn and I did everything we could to help Diana and Erick in terms of supporting them emotionally, helping with the usual household things that Diana could not do, such as grocery shopping and caring for the children. Erick loves basketball, and he needed time to decompress from the stress he felt trying to care for Diana and the children. We spent a small fortune on Spurs tickets so that he could have a few hours of respite every now and then and focus on something other than his anxiety over Diana for a few hours. Diana continued to work, through a telecommuting arrangement worked out with her Army bosses. (She worked as a civilian in NAF contracting at Ft. Sam Houston.)

The children were stressed as well but did not understand all that was happening with their mother. How do you answer a seven year old when he asks, "MorMor (what my grandchildren call me), is my Mommy going to die?" My heart was breaking for Diana, for Erick, and for the little ones. Diana began to keep a blog about her journey through surgery, chemotherapy, and later radiation. It was not only therapeutic for her but I think for all of us as we read it and commented on it. It kept us all connected on a daily basis.

Despite the long distance between us, Aryn certainly knew everything that was happening and all of us were in frequent contact with each other. At the same time, her adoptive mother had been diagnosed with a different form of breast cancer, so in a sense, Aryn was doubly stressed.

As things progressed and Diana continued her chemotherapy, Aryn decided that she needed to come to San Antonio to see Diana. She did not want Diana to know she was coming; only Elizabeth and I knew what she planned. Diana was nearing the end of her course of chemotherapy in early April, and Aryn timed her visit to occur in the first weeks of April. Diana, suffering the fatigue that goes with chemotherapy, was feeling somewhat despondent and struggling to keep herself hopeful about the outcome of chemotherapy and the soon-to-be-started radiation therapy, so Aryn's timing was perfect.

Aryn and Martin arrived on the 8th of April, and Bjorn too was surprised when they arrived because Elizabeth and I had not told him of Aryn's plans. It was a wonderful surprise for him too. He was happy that they came and was delighted to see Aryn. We found some pretext to go to Diana's, and all of us headed to her house. The plan was for Bjorn and me to go in and then say we forgot something in the car and then bring Aryn and Martin in the house. When Aryn walked in and surprised Diana, it was the best medicine anyone could have given her at that moment. The surprise, the tears, the hugs, and the laughter made us all forget for a moment the reason for the visit.

While Aryn and Martin were in San Antonio, they got married! Aryn had planned the wedding all along but had not told us that the wedding was part of the plan for the visit. So we had something to celebrate! The visit was a better boost than any medicine. Diana's spirits were lifted and she faced the radiation treatments that followed her chemotherapy with renewed energy and hopefulness. After a week-long visit, Aryn and Martin returned to Germany.

By the end of 2008, Diana's treatments were completed and, other than receiving maintenance doses of Herceptin every three weeks, life returned to some normalcy. Elizabeth had gotten engaged at the beginning of 2008 just a few days before Diana's surgery. She had given up her apartment early in the year and moved in with Diana and Erick to help them while Diana underwent her treatments. In the early summer she decided to move to Florida to be closer to her fiancé who was assigned to Patrick AFB.

Soon 2008 became 2009 and life hummed along for all of us with the usual interplay of work, school, and celebrations of birthdays and holidays. In June 2009 I accepted the position as Dean of the College of Nursing and Health Sciences at Texas A&M International University in Laredo and began weekly commutes between San Antonio and Laredo. I spent part of the week in Laredo and part in San Antonio. There were no trips across the Atlantic Ocean for us or for Aryn, so our communication continued to be what it had so often been – emails and phone calls. Our phone calls were pretty much on a weekly basis. Diana and Aryn often phoned each other as well. Diana's health remained stable with no recurrence of cancer, so life seemed to be as normal as possible. Aryn was so fully integrated into our lives and our family by then that it was hard to remember a time when she wasn't a part of the family.

The year passed quickly and soon it was 2010. Elizabeth was busy planning her wedding for July. Her fiancé Chris had been sent on a remote assignment to Thule AB, Greenland, so most of the planning and preparations for the wedding fell to Elizabeth.

Aryn was part of the wedding party and began to make plans for her trip to Florida. It was she who found us a house to rent for the week we would all be in Florida for the wedding. We drove from San Antonio, met Aryn at the Orlando airport, and spent the week doing final preparations, attending the rehearsal dinner, and just enjoying being together as a family. Our friends the Rabons arrived; Jerry was one of Chris' groomsmen. Friends and family came from near and far; some from Charleston and San Diego and New York, and Elizabeth's college classmates who were part of the wedding party arrived from Germany and Missouri. It was a full house and a jam-packed week. We left the day after the wedding to return to San Antonio, and Aryn left the following day to return to Germany. Little did we know that was to be our last really happy time together to celebrate as a family.

Several weeks prior to our departure for Florida and the wedding, Bjorn had seen the cardiologist at the 59th Medical Wing at Lackland AFB and was scheduled for a cardiac catheterization (cardiac cath or cath) the first week of August. He had the cardiac cath as scheduled and spent a night in the hospital. Based on the results of the cath, the cardiologists and the cardiac surgeons decided that he needed a quadruple bypass for an 80% blockage of his cardiac vessels. He was scheduled for surgery on 13 September at the San Antonio Military Medical Center (SAMMC). The doctors told him what the possible complications could be, particularly because he was a Type 2 diabetic. He had the surgery as scheduled and unfortunately, he had every possible complication and spent six weeks in the Cardiac Intensive Care Unit (CICU).

The cardiac surgeon told me that he never anticipated that Bjorn would have all the complications that he did. Bjorn spent several weeks on the cardiac floor once he was moved from the CICU. His kidneys had failed as a result of the surgery, so he had to begin dialysis treatments three times a week. Because his health status was so fragile, the girls – Aryn and Elizabeth – came home from Germany in December a few weeks before Christmas. (Chris had been reassigned to Ramstein AB, so now Elizabeth and Chris were living in Germany also.) Diana and Ellen were both in San Antonio. When Aryn and Elizabeth arrived, Bjorn was still at SAMMC, but after a family conference with the cardiology staff, he was transferred to a rehabilitation hospital to begin cardiac rehabilitation. He did well for a few days but then he had some complications and problems with dialysis and he was transferred to Methodist Hospital for further treatment.

At the same time that this occurred, Diana had breast reconstructive surgery and was also in the hospital. She was doing well. Aryn stayed with her one night and also visited Bjorn. With both of them in the hospital, it was a challenge taking care of the children, visiting with both of them, and carrying on with all the myriad daily activities that don't stop just because someone is in the hospital. Aryn and Elizabeth both returned to Germany just before Christmas. By that time, Diana was home from the hospital and Bjorn was back at the rehabilitation hospital.

Bjorn came home from the rehabilitation hospital in late January and did well for most of 2011. He was able to drive himself to his dialysis treatments three times a week, Aryn and Martin came for a short visit in March, and in May we flew to Charleston for a weekend when I did Cathy Hallett's promotion ceremony. In late October, he had an unresponsive episode at the dialysis clinic and had to be admitted to the hospital. He never fully recovered from that unresponsive episode. He could no longer drive, and he began to have vision problems and difficulties in remembering things – all of which distressed him greatly. His dialysis graft needed almost continual revisions, which served as an additional stressor for him. Although he had some good days, the bad days became more frequent.

When Bjorn's health became more fragile, I had resigned my dean position at the university in Laredo and begun teaching online for Texas A&M University-Texarkana, which enabled me to do everything from home and take care of Bjorn. On 12 December 2012, Bjorn wanted to go out to dinner. Since he really had no appetite for food and rarely wanted to eat, Ellen and I took him to dinner. When we returned home, I went upstairs to grade papers and they remained downstairs in the family room. I had only been upstairs a short while when I heard a horrible thud. I ran downstairs to find Bjorn unresponsive on the kitchen floor and Ellen frantic. I told her to call 911 and tried to assess Bjorn's status. The paramedics arrived within five minutes and transported him to the hospital. He never came home. He remained unresponsive and unable to communicate with us following this recent episode. He was often aware that I was with him but he could not respond. The doctors said there was nothing that could be done for him because he was going into complete system failure. We made arrangements to transfer him to hospice care.

Aryn and Elizabeth both came home from Germany. Elizabeth arrived the day before he was transferred to the hospice at Santa Rosa and Aryn arrived the day after he died. Elizabeth was with him the night he died, and for awhile he was able to talk to her and knew that Aryn was on her way. I was not there that night because my encounter with the trash bin a week earlier had left me with a fractured wrist and a fractured ankle and I was not very mobile without a great deal of assistance.

Bjorn died on 10 January 2013. He would have loved his funeral – a perfect blend of a reverent and prayerful liturgy and religious and military pageantry. His Fourth Degree Knights of Columbus Assembly provided the Honor Guard and the USAF Honor Guard did the flag folding ceremony and played Taps. The prayers at the wake the night prior to the funeral were led by our friend from Air Force days, Jim Hewson, who is now a permanent deacon in San Antonio. Aryn and Erick both spoke from their hearts about what it meant to be a part of Bjorn's life and family. Several days after the funeral, Aryn and Elizabeth returned to Germany. All of us were left with our memories of a beloved husband, father and grandfather. Every time I look at the pictures from Elizabeth's wedding, I recall how happy that time was for all of us. It was the last occasion that Bjorn was able to truly enjoy with his family.

I cannot put into words my grief at losing Bjorn. We were married four weeks short of 38 years. We had a very happy marriage and I wasn't ready for it to end. I think I could write a book about all the joys and sorrows we experienced throughout those nearly 38 years. Bjorn was a hopeless romantic who loved me and his children and family unconditionally and passionately. I will always grieve and I will always miss him.

Aryn:

Life, and my role within the Aune family, had taken on a comfortable familiarity. I visited San Antonio when possible and frequently called or stayed in touch. As an indoctrinated member of the Aune clan, I had no idea we would share in some of the most difficult chapters in our lives. Families often share the experiences of graduations, weddings and births, but for a few years we carried the heavy burden of both sickness and death.

Shortly after Christmas in 2008, I would learn that Diana had breast cancer. She was only 30, with four small children. She was terrified. We spoke in our normal, direct fashion and I simply cut to the chase.

"I won't ask if you're okay, because I know you are not. Just tell me what I can do," I pleaded during one of our conversations. We talked at length about her fears and her greatest concern that this disease would keep her from seeing her children grow up. Diana's cancer was aggressive. She and her doctors decided a double mastectomy was her best course of treatment, with chemo and radiation to follow. My distance was a heavy burden. I did not know how to help and support with so many miles between us. I felt helpless.

Helpless is not a feeling I am comfortable with, nor am I willing to accept it. I wanted to anticipate Diana's needs. I wanted to find a way to help her get through in any way I could. As the news washed over me, my mind searched frantically for ways to help. I could not help her medically; my distance would prevent me from helping in any practical way. I was at a loss. The only course of action I knew was to find ways to let her know she was loved and I would be there.

Within 24 hours, I booked a flight to San Antonio for the coming weeks, but my plan was to surprise Diana. She was about to face the fight of her life and I just wanted to find some way to give her strength and remind her she was loved from the across the ocean. I quickly enlisted the help of SA Mom, and the plans were in place.

There are a handful of moments where you know your decision was just the right choice. We picked up pizza and our plan was that I would wait at the door as a delivery person. I stood anxiously outside her house. When the door opened, Diana was in complete shock. She hugged me fiercely, and together tears streamed down our faces. She was in for the fight of her life and I would be there.

Diana is a fighter and never gives up. Now, seven years later, her cancer has been in remission for years, but she still has periodic treatments and still remains vigilant over her health. She amazes me.

★ ★ ★

As the years passed with lightning speed, by summer of 2010 we had brighter moments to celebrate as I returned stateside to celebrate Elizabeth's wedding. As a bridesmaid, I shared in another milestone family event. We danced, we celebrated, and we created lifetime memories. What was particularly significant about Elizabeth's wedding was that SA Dad was in good health. He beamed as he shared the father/daughter dance. We shared this event perfectly together as family.

Shortly after Elizabeth's wedding, SA Dad was scheduled for a medical procedure. He had a few medical issues he was monitoring, but he always downplayed any concerns, and it seemed there was little reason to worry.

And then there was nothing but worry. After SA Dad's procedure, things took a drastic turn. He was scheduled for a cardiac catheterization, which then resulted in a quadruple bypass. While I did not understand any of the medical jargon, in October I was on my way stateside again. There were concerns that his health had deteriorated to such an extent, SA Dad may need hospice care.

Upon my arrival, I was faced with the situation of feeling helpless again. I jumped in and began to organize and prioritize. I spent hours by SA Dad's bedside and chatted when he felt well enough. Mostly, I sat next to him with his hand in mine, letting him know he was loved.

The doctors quickly changed his prognosis and indicated he could receive significant rehabilitation. The next step was to maneuver through the insurances and paperwork requirements to begin his treatment. Life had its way of moving with some predictability, but the moment health issues launched to the forefront, the world stopped and there was no chance to grasp onto routine.

By the time I had returned to Germany, rehabilitation had begun and SA Dad was building his determination to get back to life as he knew it. For a time he was able to return to many of his former activities, but the damage he incurred was irreversible and there was an uphill battle ahead.

SA Mom was balancing a commute working as the nursing dean in Laredo, Texas. She was living in Laredo throughout the week and commuting home for the weekends. This, in conjunction with SA Dad's failing health, was a heavy burden.

In November of 2012, SA Dad fell, and it set a series of dominos into motion. His health quickly deteriorated and he was forced to stay in the hospital. To add insult to injury, SA Mom was on her way for a visit with him and fell, breaking her wrist and ankle. It felt like the storms were upon us. Calls stateside were frequent as I tried to keep up with the latest concerns and health updates.

By January, SA Dad's outlook was grim. I began making arrangements to return stateside. I had my flight booked and scheduled, but sadly on January 10, 2013, SA Dad passed away. I did not make it in time. I returned for the funeral and spent the flight with heavy heart as I reminisced the previous 12 years since we had met.

While my relationship began with SA Mom because of Operation Babylift and the C-5, SA Dad quickly became a driving force in my incorporation into the family. He offered me nothing but kindness and love, opening his heart and home to me without hesitation. The unique bond I had forged with the Aune family was not possible without the unwavering support of SA Dad and each of their daughters.

SA Dad always had a smile, a teasing joke and a warm hug to offer. He spent a lifetime supporting SA Mom following her career wherever it took them. As I stood before the closest friends and family to speak at his funeral, my voice began clear but soon cracked as I fought back emotions and struggled to push through my last loving thoughts.

The book had slowed in progress through those years, but before SA Dad's health deteriorated he remained vigilant, always encouraging us and wanting us to take the time to write. His presence was often with us as we searched for words to tell our unique story. Losing SA Dad was one more reason that writing now seemed more important than ever. A year later plans were in motion for us to return to Vietnam and to close the loop on Operation Babylift.

11

Sisters

Regina:

When Aryn and I began to work on writing this book, Diana commented to us that the three of them – Ellen, Diana, and Elizabeth – should have a chapter to write their thoughts about how Aryn came to be such a vital and integral part of the Aune family. Though she said it somewhat in jest, Aryn and I decided it would be good to let each of them make some comments. Without any commentary from either Aryn or me, what follows are each of their comments. Because Aryn and I know them so well, we can say what they wrote and how they wrote their comments truly reflects each of their personalities.

Ellen:

"The Lady Was A Tiger" – I will always remember that title of an article. My intimidating loving mom! I spent years thinking I had to live up to her abilities. I know now she will teach me those abilities. She has inspired me with her boundless love and her abilities. Aryn is just the right addition to our family. I am always cautious about allowing anyone into the family, though not anywhere nearly as cautious as Diana, the family pit bull. Aryn is my sister. No questions!

Diana:

Mom and Aryn asked us girls to write a chapter in their book, and I had a little difficulty at first. I mean, the reflection of their lives and the ongoing journey they continue to travel is so important that I did not think I could add anything of significance, but here I am, at the last minute putting on paper my memories of life with Mom and getting a new sister as an adult.

I honestly do not remember how old I was when Mom was sworn back into the Air Force, probably around eight, but I remember thinking she was pretty cool. People took pictures and they ended up being in the newspaper (pretty sure Mom has a clip of it somewhere). I knew Mom had been in Vietnam – I knew she had been in a plane crash, she had lost a good friend and saved a bunch of babies while she was hurt. I did not realize the significance of all she had been through until I grew older. Mom spoke about the plane crash at times, although she was very technical in the delivery of what happened, so as a child I did not think about the emotional aspects to overcoming that type of trauma. As an adult, I realize surviving that ordeal and living through the years dealing with the memories and emotions in such a positive way is awe-inspiring. My mom is awesome.

When we were growing up, Mom always opened the doors of our house to all of our friends. Ellen, Elizabeth and I had sleepovers and friends at our house all the time – so much so that when she left her teaching assignment at the School of Aerospace Medicine, a parting gift was a caricature of Mom running around doing the 101 things she managed to do for work, and us calling and telling her we were having a sleepover at our house. The caricature was drawn in such a way that she looked stressed out! When we were in San Antonio the first time in the late 80s and early 90s, my friend Esme lived with her dad, and her mother lived in South America so Mom let her stay at our house many times and sort of took her in as an honorary Aune girl. Mom always welcomed kids with open arms, so it was not surprising when, in 2001, I learned that she had met one of the 'babies' from the plane – Aryn. Mom and Aryn had connected and quickly developed a strong bond.

The summer of 2001, my two children, Makayla and Anthone, and I were staying with Mom and Dad for a couple months while my husband Erick was attending Army Recruiter School at Fort Jackson, South Carolina. I thought it was really cool for Mom to have met and begun a relationship with Aryn, but I really started to see how important Aryn was to her when she became upset one day while we were there. Mom explained that Aryn was in the process of moving to New Mexico and someone had stolen Aryn's things out of the car/trailer. I remember thinking that was terrible about Aryn's things being stolen, but why was it such a big deal to Mom? At the end of that summer, Mom and Dad moved to New Mexico as well, since mom had gotten orders to serve as the Medical Group Commander at Kirtland AFB. She was looking forward to being able to see more of Aryn. What makes Mom happy made me happy, so I had no worries… Aryn was just a friend.

Over the course of the next several months, I would hear more and more of Aryn. Erick, Makayla, Anthone and I went to visit Mom and Dad over Christmas and were able to meet Aryn face to face. By that time, unbeknownst to Aryn, she had solidified her place in our crazy Aune family… whether she liked it or not! I could tell Aryn was not quite sure how she fit, if she fit, and if we three girls were ok with her. There was some awkwardness at first but the acceptance was just that. If Mom and Dad opened their arms, hearts and home to Aryn, we just had to accept that. If anyone has ever met Mom, there is Regina and there is Colonel Aune and sometimes Colonel Aune comes out and makes decisions we all follow!

Mom always 'gave' us opportunities to develop a relationship with Aryn over the following years. We all partied together when Elizabeth graduated from college – nothing like Ellen, Aryn and I bonding over food, alcohol and tormenting Elizabeth! I am always protective of Mom, so once I determined that Aryn was not just trying to get a piece of the inheritance, we were good. Seriously.

In 2004, I was pregnant with Amiyah when Mom received orders to deploy to Kuwait. If there was any question whether Aryn belonged to Mom, it was squelched when mom drew up her will. Mom had outlined some things for Dad and all four of us girls – the four of us… not the three Aune girls. Aryn may not have had an official adoption paper with Mom's name, but Mom made certain that they would forever be linked officially on paper. This was another Colonel Aune move. Decision made, move on. And yes, it was the right decision.

In time, we sisters found it unnecessary for Mom to give us the opportunities to be together with Aryn – we wanted to see each other. When Aryn graduated with her Master's degree, she wanted us all to be there, so we were. Amiyah had been born by then, so we had more introductions to make. This time Aryn and I spent more time developing our relationship; Aryn was going through some tough times and, if nothing else, tough times strengthen bonds. I decided Mom hadn't made a rash decision and once again, she was right to envelop Aryn into our family. Over the years, we spent as much time together as possible, despite the fact all parts of the family were dispersed across the states at different military bases.

In 2005, Mom, Dad, Elizabeth, Erick, the kids and I were all living in San Antonio. Aryn was still in New Mexico dealing with difficulties when she called me one morning. I remember driving into work when I got the call and she was very upset, and needed to talk about some things but was worried how I would react. I told her that it really didn't matter what she told me, it would not change our relationship, that I loved her no matter what. And that was that. I am my mother's daughter after all. I think Aryn needed to hear that from me. Elizabeth always wears her heart on her sleeve, can make a friend with almost everyone so she was an 'easy' one to win over. I am not. If I had any hesitation about Aryn, I would have made it known, and Aryn knew this.

Erykah was born September 28, 2006. This was important because Colonel Aune had her retirement ceremony scheduled for October 6, and we had to make sure Erykah was here by then so everyone could meet her. Yes, I jokingly say this was another Colonel Aune decision. Aryn had moved to Germany by then and brought home the Bavarian Mr. Clean (aka Martin) to meet us as well. As mom's military career came to a close, I started to reflect on how her career had impacted my life in more than just how many moves we made growing up. That plane crash in Vietnam had brought another sister into my life, another aunt for my kids and, over the years, healing to Mom. I was so glad Mom had her; she is as much a piece of Mom as Ellen, Elizabeth and I are.

In 2008, I was diagnosed with breast cancer, which was startling and devastating. I was 30. As hard as that was on me, I could not imagine how hard that must have been on Mom. I do not know what she felt or how she dealt with all of it; I can barely remember how I managed to get through it. Elizabeth moved in with us to help Erick take care of the kids and me. One day, Mom came over to the house and brought with her a surprise for me. Aryn was there, and all I remember is hugging her and crying.

As much as we accepted Aryn as our sister, she had accepted us as her sisters too. Aryn came for a visit, but she brought Martin with her and they were married here in San Antonio. I was able to be a witness and was so honored! (Martin is this big muscle guy that has infiltrated the family and demands steak every time he comes to Texas!)

When dad was really sick, Aryn came home and supported us. Being the type A person that she is, she organized lists and started bossing people around. When he passed away, Aryn spoke at his wake. If anyone outside the family questioned her place in our lives, it stopped then.

A tragedy occurred on April 4, 1975. Nations mourned the loss of innocent lives, families lost loved ones, and survivors were left to pick up the pieces. I could never imagine what that felt like for Mom – to live with the memories of that day. I also could never imagine the questions Aryn lives with regarding her country of birth and how she fits. I believe that both Aryn and Mom have been searching for 'normal' in the years since the crash. Maybe one day they will learn that there is no normal, but until then, I am happy they are searching together as mom and daughter.

Elizabeth:

Growing up, I knew that my mom was part of Operation Babylift; however I did not realize how it would impact my life as a young adult. I knew that Mom was instrumental in helping to save the lives of many babies, and I was very proud of her for that. As a child and teenager, I was very aware of the fact that my mom could have died in the plane crash, and often times I tried to spend some extra time with her; however, I did not think much about the babies on the plane. I know that seems selfish, but at the time the babies were an abstract idea, but my mom was my mom and somebody who was very real to me. Even as I grew older and went off to college, I did not think much about the babies.

Ironically, even though I was growing up, I always thought of the babies on the plane as babies, not realizing that they grew up. However, one day I heard that Mom had gotten a call from one of the "babies" on the plane. That was the first time I stopped and thought about it and realized the "babies" were now young adults, and in fact they all were older than I was. I thought it was cool that one of the "babies" wanted to get in touch with Mom and I was sure Mom liked it. When I heard that she and Mom were able to get together for dinner and even had sent some emails back and forth, I also thought that was pretty neat, but I didn't think much more of it.

Between my sophomore and junior years of college, my mom got reassigned to Albuquerque, New Mexico. My mom was reassigned at the time that Aryn also made the decision to move to New Mexico to be with her fiancé. During my junior year of college, whenever I talked to Mom or got an email from her I was hearing her mention Aryn more and more. I once again thought it was nice that Mom was getting to know one of the orphans from the plane. When I got home for Christmas that year, my mom suggested that Aryn and I get together for coffee. I agreed to meet Aryn, thinking that I would have coffee with her and that would be that, never realizing that meeting for coffee that night was the beginning of a relationship. I basically agreed to meet Aryn for coffee because I knew that if I didn't Mom would keep bugging me until I agreed and, from what Mom said, Aryn seemed like a nice person. Aryn and I went out for coffee and ended up talking for close to three hours. Later on, Aryn admitted that Mom had warned her I could be a chatter box at times, but I would like to point out that Aryn kept up with me in the conversation!

Aryn and I hit it off right away. During that first Christmas break and any other time I came home to Albuquerque on a school break it became common for Aryn and me to hang out, or for the whole family to go out together. Even as Aryn and I were becoming closer, I also knew that she and Mom were becoming closer too, which did not bother me. I don't remember the first time that I heard Aryn call my parents "Mom and Dad," but it did not shock me, as I knew how much my parents cared for Aryn and vice versa.

By the time I graduated from college and moved to Boston for my first nursing job, Aryn was definitely part of the family. While the three original Aune sisters were fine with it, I think Aryn sometimes worried that we still did not view her as a sister. I remember before Mom deployed to Kuwait during Operation Iraqi Freedom, she redid her will. For me, it was hard knowing that she even did a will, but the contents of the will did not upset me. But I do remember getting an almost frantic call from Aryn to let us know that she did not know or even think that Mom was going to put her in her will. I remember thinking to myself, "Why is she so upset? She is our sister now, of course she would be in the will."

Through the years my bond with Aryn has only gotten stronger as we have both celebrated together and cried together. Some of the happier memories are Aryn being there to celebrate Mom and Dad's anniversary when Mom got home from Kuwait, seeing Aryn and Martin get married when they came to Texas to visit us, visiting Aryn and Martin in Garmisch on my trip to Germany, and Aryn being part of the wedding party when Chris and I got married. Aryn was also there when Dad was seriously ill in the hospital and when he passed away.

I know when I introduce Aryn as my sister, I get some questioning looks, as we look nothing alike. While Aryn is not my "legal" sister, nor my biological sister, she is my sister of the heart. Some people have wondered if I am jealous of the relationship that Aryn has with my mother, and I am not jealous for two main reasons. One, I have realized that Mom has a big heart and just because she loves Aryn doesn't mean that she loves me any less. Also, while I know that Mom and Aryn have a special relationship, I know it does not change the special relationship that I have with my mom.

12

Closing the Loop

Regina:

The story we have written has been gestating in our minds and hearts for many years. When we first talked about writing the book, we both knew that we couldn't write it without going to Vietnam. As we planned our strategy for writing the book, we also planned the trip. Originally, we wanted to go to Vietnam sooner, but the timing never seemed to work for us until this past year. In spring 2014, I went to Germany and we began to write our story and make final plans for the trip. Aryn, the ever resourceful organizer, found a villa to rent for the two weeks we were going to be in Vietnam. We asked Ray Snedegar if he would like to join us on the trip and, much to our delight, he said "Yes!" He would come with us.

As eagerly as we planned the trip, and even though I very much wanted to go, there was a part of me that vacillated and was hesitant about going. I quite honestly didn't know what to expect, and perhaps even more to the point, I didn't know how I would respond emotionally to being in Vietnam once again. My last time in Vietnam was a horrible day of tragedy that altered my life in many ways. I did not want this trip to be the same. My thoughts and feelings as the four of us traveled to the Munich airport were a mixture of equal measures of eager anticipation, fear, anxiety, and delight – surely a strange brew of feelings and emotions! What set this trip apart from many of the other trips I have taken was that this was not a vacation in the true sense of a vacation but rather a journey back in time, as well as a journey forward into the future. I am not even sure I can articulate the reasons why returning to Vietnam was so important to me, but it was very important despite my trepidation and hesitation. I didn't know how the trip might change me, or change Aryn, Ray, or Martin.

Because of the events of 4 April 1975, I have always felt connected to Vietnam despite the fact that I really know nothing of Vietnamese culture, cannot speak the language, and know nothing of its history save what I know about the Vietnam War and U.S. involvement in it. I have met a number of Americans who are of Vietnamese heritage and some who immigrated to the U.S. in addition to the adoptees brought to the U.S. in Operation Babylift, and so I have gleaned a little of what it means and is like to be Vietnamese.

The trip was not all focused on visiting the crash site or finding one's roots; we did do some "touristy" things and enjoyed playing the tourist at times. We seemed to intersperse the frivolous with the serious and thereby balanced the trip between a vacation of sorts and learning about Vietnam and its people.

There were days during the trip when I wondered why I had come and really didn't want to be there, and there were other days I found positively exhilarating and loved every minute. I never quite knew which way I was going to experience the day; this not knowing left me off-balance. Some days I experienced at the same time both exhilaration of being in Vietnam and the desire to be someplace else – anywhere but Vietnam. The times when I was with Aryn on our shopping excursions, getting measured and fitted for our custom made ao dais (the traditional Vietnamese dress) or drinking coffee at Starbucks while the music playing was Bing Crosby singing "White Christmas" (a somewhat dissonant experience!) were especially poignant for me and I treasure those moments in particular. (Incredibly, this was the secret song that served as the signal within the military to be played on Armed Forces Radio to alert all military that the final evacuation of all Americans was underway.) That is not to say that I didn't enjoy the times when all four of us were doing things together or the times when Ray and I spent time in Ho Chi Minh City eating at McDonald's and taking pictures under the Baskin Robbins sign while Aryn and Martin were in Malaysia, because I did enjoy them.

I am still grieving my husband's death, though I hope gracefully, and I missed him terribly during the trip. Vietnam and Operation Babylift were part of our life from the very beginning of our marriage and throughout the whole 38 years we were married. Not to have him with me on this return trip left me with a gaping, aching giant hole in my heart. I had some truly bad days while I was in Vietnam, but I tend always to try to hide and keep out of sight my difficult days – even keeping them from those who are closest to me. On most days I found myself wishing that Bjorn were with me.

But, the trip was not a disappointment to me. And, yes, I would go back again and would like to go back again. It is four months since our return from Vietnam and though I am mentally and emotionally still processing what the trip meant to me and how it affected me, there are some thoughts that I can share. As I write these words, it is Holy Saturday, the eve of the most important Christian holy day – the Feast of the Resurrection of the Lord. It seems an odd juxtaposition – the 40th anniversary of a horrific plane crash that left 138 people dead in the muck and mud and debris in the rice paddies of Saigon, leaving the hopes of so many shattered on the shards of a wrecked plane, happening only the day before the joyous celebration of the resurrection of the Lord from the dead after his horrific passion and death on the cross. Easter has always hovered over the C-5 crash. When it occurred 40 years ago, it was Easter Friday – a mere five days after the joyous celebration of the feast. But there is a poignancy to the relationship of the two events. Death does not have the last word. Death did not have the last word on Calvary and it did not in the rice paddies of Saigon.

As I reflect on the trip in retrospect, I realize I have come full circle. While in some ways, I relived the entire experience of that one day of my life during the whole trip in Vietnam, I also lived it with Aryn and so it was infused with a happiness and joy that I did not anticipate fully. For 40 years the C-5 tragedy remained an open wound in my heart. Certainly, it had healed so that it was no longer a gaping, open wound oozing sorrow and sadness and loneliness, but it was still a wound. It was a sorrow that I carried always with me though often and always hidden from others.

Aryn came into my life late and after a long labor of questioning, wondering, and hoping. In an earlier chapter I said that there always lingered the question of whether what had happened made a difference and whether anyone cared. It was a niggling question that always existed in my mind and heart. Aryn was the answer I was given. She was an answer I never expected. Aryn and the trip we took together perfectly exemplify a quotation from St. Therese that I take great comfort in reflecting upon:

"The time may be delayed, the manner may be unexpected, but the answer is sure to come. Not a tear of sacred sorrow, not a breath of holy desire, poured out to God will ever be lost, but in God's own time and way will be wafted back again in clouds of mercy, and fall in showers of blessings on you, and on those for whom you pray."

Aryn came to me in God's own time and brought with her the blessings of her presence in my life, another daughter to love and whom in many ways I had always loved without knowing her.

One of my greatest anxieties in departing on the trip was the fear that all of us would be changed in some way and perhaps those unknown changes would alter our relationship. The trip did change us, but not in any negative way. Sharing our adventure, uncovering the past, pursuing the present and looking to the future deepened the relationships among us, particularly my relationship with Aryn. She is as much a part of my life as are Ellen, Diana, and Elizabeth and she always will be.

In looking at the trip in light of the 40 years that have elapsed since the crash and Operation Babylift, life was born out of the ashes of tragedy, hope triumphed over despair, love trumped hate, and joy displaced sorrow. Although God's hand was invisible, his Divine Providence was always present. One of my favorite poems is "God's Granduer," by Gerard Manley Hopkins, SJ. Although I love the whole poem, the last line is especially meaningful to me and illuminates what I am trying to convey much better than I can: ". . . Because the Holy Ghost over the bent world broods with warm breast and with ah! bright wings."

Despite what I said earlier about my fears, hesitations, and anxiety over the trip, I am very, very glad that I went.

Aryn:

We began to plan our trip in May of 2014. SA Mom had come to visit and we were beginning the process of writing our book. As we tucked ourselves away in seclusion, we reached back to tell the story of how our paths had crossed, separated, and come together again as one.

SA Mom continued to work through the grief of losing SA Dad. She was heavy-hearted that he would not share in this lifelong dream. As we began to plan, SA Mom had a revelation. I had recently met up with Ray Snedegar on a trip to Ohio. He too had survived that fateful day of April 4th and had recently attended a reunion in California. We had not seen one another since 2006, but our connection was instantaneous. Together we laughed, we shared stories and talked in depth about the reunion and how he was amazed by the adoptees and their stories.

126

"We should invite Ray to come to Vietnam." SA Mom continued, "I think it would be amazing if we could all share in this experience." I loved the idea and we immediately called Ray.

Without a single moment of hesitation, he graciously accepted. I marveled that not only was this trip moving forward, but all of the pieces were falling into place. I would be traveling back to my homeland with two survivors of the C-5.

In November of 2014, after 40 years, the time had come. I was returning to Vietnam. With my husband, SA Mom, and Ray, we left from Munich, Germany to start our adventure. After 18 long hours we finally arrived in Vietnam.

I had lived in Germany for the past nine years and travelled throughout Europe. I took the opportunity to live overseas to travel and see the world. My love for photography had grown and I took advantage of every opportunity to capture the culture and landmarks in the cities I visited. When I first began traveling, it was the most amazing natural high. I felt truly alive in those moments and soaked up every experience. Over time, while I still enjoyed the experience of traveling, the high was not as intense – until Vietnam.

We made our approach into Saigon in the evening hours. I stared intensely out the window in awe as we approached the city. Little lights moved along the streets like fireflies buzzing about. I could feel the adrenaline and the excitement building. The natural high was back and I could not wait to see my homeland. Despite the long flight, I didn't feel an ounce of fatigue.

Gathering all of our belongings, we deplaned and headed for the main terminal. I exited and one of the flight attendants looked at me and said, "Welcome home." I was taken aback and as I walked through the door, I looked back to my husband questioningly, "Did he just say 'Welcome Home'?" A woman within earshot looked at me and said, "He didn't say it to me."

I walked the ramp with the widest smile. Maybe I was reading into things too much, but all I could think was how perfectly fitting.

After we maneuvered through the chaotic visa process, we were finally ready to start our adventure. The moment we walked outside, my glasses fogged and I was hit with a wall of heavy, humid air. I could hear chatter all around me in Vietnamese. Unable to understand a single word, the sounds struck me as nasally and high pitched. I immediately located the driver holding a sign with my name and we headed towards the villa I had arranged for our stay.

To describe the drive to our villa as chaotic would be an understatement. Our driver spoke no English so we chatted amongst ourselves marveling at the traffic and the near collisions we saw from moment to moment. The streets were filled with scooters weaving in and out of traffic. There appeared to be no rules, no order. There was a consistent melody of scooters and cars honking as we inched our way out of the city. I gazed upon two, three, four people per scooter, all maneuvering stealthily to get to their destinations. They drove within mere inches of one another without being fazed at all. The honking was merely a notification of their presence. There was no hint of aggravation or frustration from the scores of drivers around us. A quick maneuver to the left, to the right, and on they continued.

Once we were outside of the city, we were on the highway headed towards district two. The traffic separated into scooters on the side road and cars on the main thoroughfare. We took a variety of twists and turns making our way to the villa. As we came closer, I remarked upon the poor conditions. The streets were dirty and littered. When we finally arrived, I immediately noticed the massive iron gate and barbed wire that surrounded the perimeter. I began to wonder if I had chosen a safe neighborhood.

We were greeted by my interpreter, Nhu, and Mrs. Thanh, the caretaker of the residence. Nhu was quite young. She was petite in stature and welcoming as she handed me a cell phone and explained that I could reach her at any time. She provided us with keys to the residence and answered any questions we had. Mrs. Thanh was much older and spoke with a heavy accent. She stayed on the grounds and was available to us throughout our stay.

The villa was breathtaking. As I prepared our trip, I wanted to find a place where we could all have privacy, but also spend time together. I was concerned a hotel with individual rooms would be too separate. We were embarking on a life-changing journey, and how we spent our downtime together was equally as important as what we would see. The villa was decorated impeccably. We walked through the large front doors into a massive open living room with 20 foot ceilings. This was amazing. The advertisement photos failed to do this villa justice.

We began to discuss our itinerary. I purposely did not want to cram our time with planned events for every day. We had two full weeks and plenty of time to ensure we saw what was most important. We had decided our first destination would be the crash site. We did not have an exact location, but hoped we could find the coordinates through the internet as other adoptees had visited the site in the past. Nhu would be joining us the next day and she was amazingly helpful. She was intrigued by our story and was invaluable as she helped us with the language barrier and with uncovering information.

We arranged a driver and prepared to find the crash site the next morning. It took some time, but eventually we made our way to District 12. It seemed every destination we travelled to took much longer than I anticipated. Because of the chaos and traffic, going just a few miles took close to an hour.

As we travelled, I could not stop observing. Scooters passed by with sleeping children, standing children, puppies, and the women were covered from head to toe despite the sweltering temperatures. Nhu explained that women took extreme measures to avoid the sun and did not want to appear tan. In Vietnam, "It is a different beauty standard." Safety standards were not only different – they were nonexistent. Telephone poles were a mess of wires and entangled in complete chaos. Crossing the street was a game of chicken. It appeared to me, the slightest wrong move and you were doomed. It was survival of the fittest and most courageous.

As we neared closer to District 12, Nhu and our driver stopped frequently to ask locals about our destination. We waited patiently, hoping we were getting closer. In the car, out of the car, chat with this local, chat with that local. I noticed there were frequently people standing or sitting around the local shops. One of our last destinations was a barbershop on the side of the road. The barber inspected the paper Nhu held as he sat outside of his shop. Though there were no customers, hair littered the floor, looking unkept and unhygienic. This was the Vietnamese standard.

After almost two hours of searching, Nhu reported back to us, "It's just up the road." We got out of the car next to a field and walked a narrow path to a clearing. Nhu explained it was here that other adoptees had returned yearly. We had searched online looking for images from other adoptees who had visited the site. Based on the pictures we had found online, this looked right. To the left of us was a building and in front a field of dark green vegetation and a stream of water. Two workers were in the field as we surveyed the area. There were no markings and no indication this was where the accident had occurred. I imagined there was at least a small plaque, or some shrine to mark the events of April 4th so many years ago; 40 years prior this was nothing but rice fields. The small businesses and the road were nonexistent. I had a difficult time relating to this empty field, trying to imagine wreckage and the aftermath of the horrific crash. As we stood within the field, we heard planes approaching behind us. This was still the flight path of the airport.

Upon surveying the incoming planes, Ray stated, "This is definitely it. We were on the approach towards Tan Son Nhut when we crashed a couple of miles from the runway." As he watched the planes pass behind us, I saw his eyes begin to well up. There was silence among us. I imagined that both Ray and SA Mom were experiencing something very different than I. They survived; they remembered standing in this field among twisted metal, the shattered remnants of the aircraft and the painful loss of life. At this point, I was unsure of my role, but I still felt strongly connected. My love for both my SA Mom and Sister Ursula ensured the indelible link to the field before me.

During our two weeks in Vietnam, we visited this area three times. We made the decision to return for Veteran's Day, as it felt like the best way to honor both SA Mom, Ray and the fallen from the C-5 tragedy.

On our second pilgrimage to the crash site, we did not have our interpreter with us and we had a new driver. Traveling throughout Europe, you can often find some way to get through as an English speaker, but in Vietnam, I was relegated to basic hand gestures and repeating words in English as they looked upon me dazed and confused. At least I had the cell phone and Nhu was wonderfully responsive. After picking up some flowers and incense to take with us, we began our journey. As some landmarks began to look familiar, it felt like we were not exactly in the right area. I called Nhu frequently and she talked with the driver to give him better clarification. We couldn't exactly put an address into a GPS and find our way. Patience was our best companion.

The driver stopped frequently to speak to the locals, but we had no idea if we were getting closer or if we were several streets away. I had no sense of direction or my bearings. Finally, after what seemed an hour of going in circles, the driver had us get out of the car. It looked nothing like where we had been a few days prior. I was convinced we were in the wrong place. As we were being directed in Vietnamese to follow, I started to call Nhu. I was beginning to fear we would never find it again.

As we walked along a dirt road, I was simultaneously dialing Nhu, and I continued to walk reluctantly. I was sure we had taken a wrong turn because there was no clearing anywhere around us. We found ourselves next to someone's house with a small cement shrine wedged inside their fenced gate.

I started speaking to Nhu, "This isn't the right place. This isn't where we were the other day." She calmly explained that the driver learned there are two sites. The shrine had been created many years ago on someone's private property. Tan in color, it stood about four feet tall and had a narrow rectangular opening. It had a slanted roof. Inside I could see a small vase with thin red sticks from incense that had long burned down, a few marigolds in a vase. There was also a small plate inside with a few grains of rice. I had learned in the Vietnamese culture, people would often leave gifts and offerings at shrines to remember their loved ones. I was thrilled to find an actual shrine. I felt more connected to this small building than I had the open field days prior. There was still no indication of the shrine's purpose or why it was there, but I began formulating an idea to change that.

Upon learning of the second site, we discovered the field where we stood days prior was where the front of the plane was located after the crash. This shrine was built by locals many years past, and it was where the rear of the plane was located. To our continued amazement, we also learned that this shrine was built around a piece of the wreckage. Maneuvering into the cramped space between the shrine and the fence, I could see the base of a large rusting piece of metal. How amazingly fortunate! By sheer accident, we had come upon this meaningful shrine. The home owner cared for the shrine, rebuilding and tending to it in recent years. This gesture of strangers left me grateful. So many pebbles of good fortune seemed to accompany us on this trip. It was difficult to ignore how things continued to fall into place.

Our final visit to the shrine came on our last day in Vietnam. When we first visited, I was saddened to find there was no clear indicator for its purpose. It was only through the locals that we were able to uncover this treasure. I knew immediately that I wanted to leave something to let all those who passed by know why this shrine was built. When we arrived back at the villa, I downloaded a couple of images and designed a small collage with a picture of the C-5 flight 80218 taking off and an image of the wreckage. With Nhu's help, we placed our dedication in both English and Vietnamese: "In loving memory of all those who perished on C-5A 80218 on 4 April 1975."

When we returned for our final visit to the shrine, I dressed in the traditional Vietnamese dress, the Ao Dai. I beamed with pride placing the framed image into the shine. I hoped all who would come after us would now know its purpose. This was my small contribution to honor the lives lost on that fateful day – a simple reminder that they are not forgotten.

★ ★ ★

In the initial days of my return to Vietnam, I was up frequently in the early hours. In the quiet of those hours, I watched the sun rise over my homeland and heard roosters crow. I was so completely overwhelmed, I felt like my brain was going to explode. My senses were overloaded. I attempted to store every detail fearing that I would forget.

I would sit in the car and fight back tears; I would walk the street and out of nowhere I had to fight back tears and talk the lump out of my throat. I felt like I was in one consistent, intense battle to keep from breaking down. I could feel my eyes well up at least five times during the day, and I looked away, I looked up, I fought them back. I tried not to let my mind touch whatever was bringing on the emotions. I promised myself I would process everything later. In my solitude, I did allow a periodic tear to fall. It was not the cry of relief where the flood gates opened in a cathartic release. These few tears escaped to keep the pressure from building to the point of complete meltdown.

Our trip included a few days for tourist attractions, allowing for lighter moments which were desperately needed. We often came home to Mrs. Thanh cooking us a traditional Vietnamese meal. The food was amazing and I loved that I could try traditional dishes that I would not have known if we were only going to restaurants. I had taken charge of itineraries for most of our days. I was open to keeping things fluid; however, there were a few plans that were very important to me. I wanted to visit an active orphanage and visit Vinh Long, the town where I was born.

Nhu accompanied us to the SOS Orphanage. We decided Sunday would be the best day to visit, as the children would be out of school and we could spend a few hours. We learned that Mrs. Thanh's two grandsons also lived there. Her son was unable to care for them and this was a better option. I asked Mrs. Thanh, what we could bring for the children. Her response was candy – so candy it would be. She and I walked to the local market. I looked at the unusual candy before me and asked her to just put whatever she thought they'd like into the basket. She tentatively began to grab a bag or two, but after continuing to encourage her, the basket was soon overflowing and I was getting excited.

Once we arrived at SOS, I soon learned this organization was founded by an Austrian. It appeared many of these children were not adoptable, but lived here as a small family. I didn't fully understand why, but essentially there were eight homes each with a house mother and 8-12 children. The women were not allowed to marry and this was their life's work. These restrictions made it difficult to find women to care for the children. The children lived together and at the age of 13, the boys had to move to another home. With our overflowing bag of candy, our plan was to visit a few homes.

As we came to our first home, all of the children's shoes were outside. As with many cultures, the tradition was to remove your shoes before entering the home. Here the youngest child lived. She was an eight-month-old baby, and when we walked toward the door, one of the boys was holding her. The baby had a full head of black curls and was happy and full of smiles. We entered the house to see a small living area and learned to the left were doors for the boys and girls. The boys scrambled as they gave us the tour of their room. It was impeccably clean with wooden bunk beds. There were no mattresses, only a wooden surface and a small fabric mat rolled up on each bed.

We handed out candy and through Nhu we learned more about the house. I was able to hold the baby for some time before handing her off to my husband, Martin. Looking into the sweet eyes of this baby, it was hard to keep the emotions under control. As she bounced happily on my husband's knee, I was very present in the moment. Ray asked a few questions and SA Mom was very quiet, observing. As our visit came to an end, the baby started to get fussy. Martin handed the baby to the house mother, saying, "See, she just wanted her mom." As we said our thanks and good-byes, I was barely out of the house when I could not hold back the emotions any longer.

Since the moment I stepped into Vietnam, my original perceptions, concepts, my way of life were being placed at constant odds, challenged at every turn. This time was such an intense blow, the emotions I had bottled so tightly and barely allowed to escape overflowed. The tears streamed down my face uncontrollably. I didn't say a single word, I just couldn't get them to stop for a moment. In that instant when Martin gave the baby back to the house mother, a light came on.

In my mind, I had imagined the orphanage I came from had a constant revolving door. I had led myself to believe that there were so many of us, we could never be known in any true sense or loved completely. We were living things being moved from one area to another until we were connected to a family or home.

After visiting our first house, I knew this was not the case. I immediately transcended this experience to my own and I was not just another nameless living entity. I was a child who was loved and cared for, and immediately I imagined Sister Ursula holding us with loving arms and showering kisses and warmth upon us. The tears would not stop.

I pulled myself together to visit our next home. What struck me most as we visited several homes was that each house had its own personality. The layout of each house was the same, with the small living room, kitchen and bedrooms. There was a sense of routine and family within each home. It was like visiting any neighborhood and seeing the differences in each home.

Our final house was filled with younger children. The children were mesmerized by Ray. The house mother explained the children were used to having a woman around, but they were not frequently in contact with men, so they were curious. Ray created videos and played them back on his iPad. They giggled, posed and played with true child-like wonderment. It was a home filled with brothers and sisters playing, lots of laughter and smiles. SA Mom continued to be very quiet and my husband was beginning to get restless. We spent our time and it was time to go.

Ray and I were fully engaged. We played with the children, we laughed and we were touched by their smiles and innocence. As we left the house and made our way to the gate, Ray wrapped his arm around me and we sobbed. Our bodies shook as we cried together saying we wished we could take them all home with us. I knew this day would be difficult, but I knew it was necessary for me to truly connect with my past and my home.

As I reflect further upon this day, I have a better understanding of people. What I realize is that we were four people sharing in one journey, but we were all processing it very differently. I believe the orphanage experience was very difficult for both my SA Mom and for Martin. The two people who knew me best, who I believed would be able to comfort me the most, could not. I was not angry or hurt, but I was surprised. I have come to realize both my San Antonio Mom and my husband had to work through their experience their own way, yet I was still glad they shared in that moment with me. Ray, whom I knew the least, provided amazing comfort and together we had solidified our bond.

In the following days, my itinerary included a visit to my birth town, Vinh Long. Located in the Mekong Delta, I had Googled to see the distance between Ho Chi Minh City and my province. It was only about 60 miles, but the estimated time was over two hours. The drive was tedious and slow, and this was with modern roads. I could only imagine what it was like during the height of the war and the long time it must have taken to transport babies to Saigon. I had learned that the location of the Vinh Long convent was now a government building. I wasn't allowed in, I wasn't allowed pictures, and I had no idea if anything remained from the days of the convent. Nhu had tried numerous times in the previous days to see if I could gain access, but to no avail. Once we arrived, her efforts were unrealized again.

I brought the book I had received about Vinh Long. The Annals were a collection of memories and stories of the convent during the war. It is through this book I learned Sister Ursula had been at the convent since its earliest days. I also learned this was a compound with the original purpose of taking in prostitutes and other unsavory persons and helping them to learn skills and professions. It later evolved to a facility to help educate young women and give them future skills.

This convent had seen some terrifying moments during the war. There was an air base just a half mile down the road, and many of those soldiers would spend their free time helping at the convent. As I stood outside the fence of this beautifully modern building, I wondered if anything from that time existed. I found it somewhat ironic that I was looking through a fence to the place where I had originated. It seemed oddly fitting that I had spent much of my life looking at my past through fences, unable to enter.

As we looked upon the building, a man walked up to us and began talking with Nhu. He explained that periodically they saw people like me return. He knew little about the past, but indicated his wife knew much more and she was across the street. Once again the serendipitous nature of our trip could not be ignored. Nhu helped to navigate the language barrier. The man and woman had a small stand. I didn't know what they were selling, as it appeared to be some form of certificate. She began telling me details about the convent and explaining the layout. She explained that the government tore everything down after the nuns left.

They were angry that the nuns had helped the Americans. I showed her my book and she went through each picture, pausing on Sister Ursula and saying she remembered her. This woman had taken classes within the convent as a young girl. I laughed when she described the mother superior. Nhu translated, "The Mother Superior was a big, white woman who talked with an accent." For good measure she emphasized, "very big, white woman."

I could only shake my head. What were the odds? So many perfectly timed moments, it seemed surreal or it seemed this trip was guided with boundless good fortune.

All of this good fortune erupted in perfect synchronicity with a weekend trip to Malaysia. During the planning of my trip to Vietnam, I had an opportunity to travel to Malaysia for a weekend. My husband and I had spent the entire year trying to build our small business, "Strongman Rage." We were heavily involved in the strongman sport. There is a niche following and people are usually familiar with it from late night shows where the athletes are featured pulling trucks and lifting heavy objects. We travelled the world with the Strongman Champions League (SCL), where I provided photography and wrote articles for their events. To explain briefly, Strongman Champions League organizes strongman competitions all over the world. There are 16 stages that occur throughout the year, and athletes accumulate points taking the top athletes to the finals. By sheer coincidence the finals were taking place in Kuala Lumpur, Malaysia, during the same time I had planned my Vietnam trip. The SCL director encouraged me to attend, reminding me that I could come to Malaysia for the finals and be back in Vietnam within 48 hours.

I was extremely reluctant. I had no intention of going. My business side knew it would be the best thing for us to participate, but I had spent years imagining this trip. I was concerned a trip to Malaysia in the middle of it would affect the momentum and change my focus. However, after much deliberation, we decided we had spent our entire year building the business painstakingly and this opportunity simply could not be missed.

Little did I know, this decision would be life-changing. I made the arrangements for our flights to Malaysia and broke the news to SA Mom. I knew she would be disappointed. After her arrival in Germany, she began looking at the Annals of Vinh Long again. As she read, she saw that Sister Ursula was from Malaysia and her body was returned to her home town after the crash. The book said Kajang, Malaysia was her home town. I didn't know anything about Malaysia and imagined it could not possibly be close to where I would be. A quick google search left me speechless. We were going to Kuala Lumpur. Kajang was only 12 miles away.

I began to fantasize that I might actually be able to find Sister Ursula's grave. At SA Mom's suggestion, I sent an email to the Arch Diocese of Kuala Lumpur. Within a single day, I had a response and I just stared at my computer. I had received an email from Jude Benjamin, who I would immediately learn was the nephew through marriage to Sister Ursula. This could not be happening. I had just found a needle in the world's haystack.

What occurred after this point is almost a blur. I called my adopted mother to tell her it looked as if I could visit Sister Ursula's grave, and she was as blown away as I was. I told her too, how I had found members of her family and I was going to meet them. My mother in her amazing wisdom said, "It would be wonderful if you meet her family, but know that if you can go to her grave, that is the moment between you two and only you two. Do not forget that."

Jude met us shortly after our arrival to Kuala Lumpur. I felt like I had found a long lost brother. We met at our hotel and shortly after we started talking, the tears flowed. Martin was with me and handed me a tissue. My husband is not known for his sensitive side, but I had come to realize when he handed me a tissue throughout these days, this was his way of offering his loving support.

I felt like my emotions were a pinball being thrown from one bumper to another. I was literally switching gears from photographing the finals of the strongman competition to desperately trying to process what was happening in my personal life. I was living in two worlds that weekend. Part of the reason we were in Malaysia was also to support our good friend, Martin Wildauer. He was poised and motivated to win the entire championship. As Wildauer placed the harness around his chest, he prepared to pull the bus with nothing more than a rope and his power. He took his position and pulled with all of his strength. Slowly the bus began its slow, laborious movement and after four steps, he fell to the ground. Wildauer had snapped his Achilles on the final event of the evening. Now worry and concern were intermixed into the sea of emotions I was trying to process.

Wildauer did not return from the hospital until three in the morning. When he returned, he made the decision to compete the next day despite his injury. The excitement of the competition was a continuation of the highly charged, emotional weekend. Wildauer fought through his injury in the greatest, dramatic fashion to win the championship. I cheered, screaming emphatically. Through my cheers, I had found another outlet for all of the emotions I was experiencing.

After only a couple of hours of sleep, Jude was meeting me and our plan was to visit Sister Ursula's grave. I had only the morning free before I had to switch gears to photograph the second day of the SCL finals. I was going to meet the family. I had made the last-minute decision to go alone and I'm glad I did. We picked up a few flowers, met the family at the church and we were off to the cemetery only a few blocks away. As we filed in, I was led to her grave. It was a beautiful, serene cemetery on the side of a hill. I had no idea how I would react. Would I feel any connection to this grave even though I have no memories of knowing this woman who cared for me and chose me for my parents? Would it meet the expectations I had spent a lifetime building?

I placed the flowers in the vase on her grave stone and the moment I looked up, saw her name and her death date, I sobbed. It was as if all the emotions I had attempted to bottle up flowed without end. Even as I write this, the tears still escape. This was the single most emotional moment I can remember. I could hear my mother's voice telling me, "This is the moment between you two and only you two," and the tears continued. As I stood before her, I thanked her, I told her how important she has been my entire life, and I wanted her to know how much she is loved and a part of me. I felt no attempt to stifle my tears or my pain.

I needed to understand how the connection was so instantaneous. As I reflected upon that moment, I wanted it to make sense. Looking back, I now understand. I have never felt a strong need to connect or find my biological roots. Many adoptees are now taking DNA tests with the hope of finding out more about their heritage. From my stories, I knew the likelihood was nonexistent and I have long accepted this. But Sister Ursula. She stood on high and as I sobbed before her, I realized why. I never imagined I would meet or could meet my biological mother, but Sister Ursula was like my birth mother. She was the first person I knew to care for me. She was solely responsible for sending me to my parents and it was with her love and devotion that I could live on, even though she died that horrific day. I have done some amazing things in my life, yet none as significant as this moment. In some ways, even more than returning to Vietnam, I had closed the loop on my beginnings.

Epilogue

Regina:

So, now we have come to the end of our book. But, it is not the end of our story. It is, rather, just a stop on our journey, which began in the rice paddies of Saigon on a hot, humid April day forty years ago.

For some twenty-odd years, Aryn's path and my path took different twists and turns as we navigated through our lives, never intersecting with each other. She was seeking answers and I was seeking healing. Then, one December day, a simple phone call caused those two separate paths to cross, and when they did, they ignited a spark that became a flame of friendship and then it grew to a fire driven by a bond of love and family. Nurtured by her desire to have questions answered, Aryn sought me and in her seeking brought me a joy and an answer to a question that had always lingered in my mind, a question I never thought I would have answered in my lifetime: Did the loss of so many lives in the tragedy that was the first flight of Operation Babylift have any meaning for anyone or make any difference to anyone? I always had believed that the events of that tragic day had purpose; that the crew members, the adults, and the babies that died had not died in vain. Still, the question always lingered. But, that simple phone call — a voice without a face at that moment — clearly and calmly told me yes, it mattered far beyond what even I could envision. My question was answered beyond my wildest dreams.

Aryn had dreamt of writing her story all her life. I didn't dream of writing about this story but I love to write and often find that it is easier for me to express my thoughts and wonderings and clarify my thinking through writing. I knew that at some point, I would need to write about this seminal experience of my life if I were to finally exorcise its demons. I just didn't know how or when that would be.

As our relationship grew from acquaintance to friendship to familial bond, so too did our desire to write about our experience grow in direct proportion. And so, it is now done. There is a certain sadness that we have now come to the end, as well as a certain joy that we have finally accomplished our dream. Yes, with Aryn I can say, Operation Babylift: Mission Accomplished, but it has not ended. In some ways, it is still beginning. There is so much more to this journey. Who knows where it will take us? We look forward to the rest of this journey of the hearts with eager anticipation and joyful expectation. Stay tuned!

Aryn:

Writing this book has been a lifelong dream. I always believed there was a story to tell. As I went about the business of my life, I was amazed how I took a variety of twists and turns, and yet I always found my way back to my words. With the fortieth anniversary of Operation Babylift, the timing seemed perfect.

As I reflect upon the words I have placed on these pages, I am humbled. The story was always there; we simply had to find the words to tell it. Our journey was made unique by extraordinary historical events. Out of the ashes of tragedy, we forged ahead, and through it we created our very own tale of hope and inspiration. There were no instantaneous miracles. We are very different people with vastly different perspectives and influences, and yet we forged this unbreakable bond. Much like my tentative beginnings, my relationship between my SA family was forged through time and a commitment to one another.

My beginnings were the result of deliberate choices. If there is one life lesson that I hold dearly, it is the power of choices. My life's path came cradled in the loving hands of people who made decisions on my behalf. Their life choices and sacrifices ultimately resulted in my ability to tell the story within these pages. It is with that same love and devotion that I chose to write. I feel that I have left myself open and vulnerable, but I feel courageous in the hope that others may relate to my words and to our story.

Operation Babylift was a humanitarian mission with the presidential stamp, but the work on behalf of orphans had taken place for years prior, and it continued long past the final flight. Operation Babylift itself has embodied and represented a majority of us who arrived throughout the world in the final days of Vietnam, but the adoptees rarely make that distinction amongst ourselves. The official humanitarian mission involved 33 flights sending approximately 3,000 orphans throughout the globe to start our new lives.

We embodied hope. While our lives began on the soil of war-torn Vietnam, we ventured to America, Canada, Australia, and throughout Europe to new journeys. Sometimes we struggled, sometimes we fell, but more often than not, we persevered. We grew up. We had our own families. We never forgot from where we came. Now, after forty years, I believe that there is no question: our lives define the efforts of sacrifice, loss and love. Operation Babylift has truly become a Mission Accomplished.

About the Authors

Regina Aune

Regina Aune was commissioned a first lieutenant in the Air Force in 1973 and served in both the active and reserve components of the Air Force, and in a variety of assignments including flight nurse, flight nurse instructor, nurse educator, administrator and commander throughout her 28-year military career. She retired as a colonel in December 2006. After retiring from the Air Force, she held a number of educational positions including serving as the dean of the College of Nursing and Health Sciences at Texas A&M International University in Laredo, Texas, for three years and teaching online nursing courses for Texas A&M University - Texarkana. Currently retired, she lives in San Antonio, Texas and is deciding on her next adventure in writing and travels.

Aryn Lockhart

Aryn Lockhart was born in Vinh Long, Vietnam and is an Operation Babylift adoptee. She was adopted by the Lockhart family and grew up in San Jose, CA and Woodbridge, VA. She graduated from Virginia Tech with a B.A. in Communications and minors in English and Psychology. She received her Masters in Business from Webster University. Currently, she works as a graphic designer for the George C. Marshall European Center for Security Studies located in Garmisch-Partenkirchen, Germany. In addition to her full-time work, she owns two small businesses, Bavarian Treasures and Strongman Rage. When she's not working, writing, or running businesses, she travels the world photographing landscapes or the strongman sport. She's married to Matthias Martin and has two step daughters.

142